THE TRACTION LIBRARY

Want even better results and more business success?

Equip every person on your team with the right information and tools to run your organization on EOS®, the Entrepreneurial Operating System®. With the Traction Library, everyone in the company—from leadership to management to employees—will understand their role and be empowered to help your company succeed.

HERE'S HOW:

For Everyone

For Entrepreneurs, Leaders and Managers

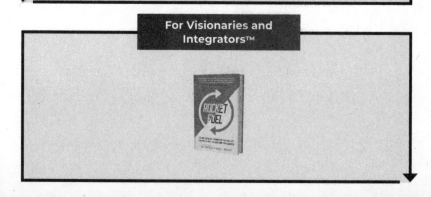

For Visionaries and Integrators™

PROCESS!

HOW DISCIPLINE AND CONSISTENCY WILL SET YOU AND YOUR BUSINESS FREE

MIKE PATON AND LISA GONZÁLEZ

BenBella Books, Inc.
Dallas, TX

BenBella Books, Inc.
10440 N. Central Expressway
Suite 800
Dallas, TX 75231
benbellabooks.com
Send feedback to feedback@benbellabooks.com

BenBella is a federally registered trademark.

Printed in the United States of America
10 9 8 7 6 5 4 3 2 1

Library of Congress Control Number: 2022013467
ISBN 9781637741368 (hardcover)
ISBN 9781637741375 (electronic)

Copyediting by Ginny Glass
Proofreading by Jenny Bridges and Cape Cod Compositors, Inc.
Text design and composition by Aaron Edmiston
Cover design by David Fassett / Notch Design
Illustrations by Drew Robinson Spork Design
Printed by Lake Book Manufacturing

To Kate, whose very existence reminds me what's possible.
—*Paton*

To Paddy, Donny, Alex, and Skyler, I love you more than the most.
—*Lisa*

If you are a reader who is not familiar with the Entrepreneurial Operating System (EOS), *Traction*, or the EOS Tools, don't worry. We've written this book so that it will bring real value to you and your business, regardless of your level of EOS understanding. If you want to learn more about EOS and the EOS Tools, we encourage you to read *Traction: Get a Grip on Your Business*, and the other books in the Traction Library. At no cost, you can also download many of the EOS Tools mentioned in this book at eosworldwide.com/eos-tools.

CONTENTS

SECTION III: ACT

FOREWORD

Are you controlling your business, or is your business controlling you? Sadly, most entrepreneurial leaders are being controlled by their businesses, and it doesn't have to be that way. You deserve to be free.

I obsess about freedom, for myself and for others who have the courage, the drive, and the work ethic to build something great and—at the same time—be *truly* free.

I've spent my entire adult life trying to prove it's possible. It started with intensive study, a relentless drive to understand the art and science of running a truly great business. I then applied what I was learning in my own family business and shared the stuff that worked best with other entrepreneurs in my network. Through painstaking trial and error, I gradually discovered six keys to running a great business and worked hard to discover the simplest and best way to strengthen those six key components in an entrepreneurial business. Out of this obsession came EOS (the Entrepreneurial Operating System). Today, EOS has a global following that includes more than five hundred EOS Implementers helping tens of thousands of companies around the world run on EOS. It's been a labor of love, borne of my desire to be free and to help others achieve that freedom as well.

There were some surprising discoveries along the way, and one of them is explored deeply by my friends and colleagues Mike Paton and Lisa González in this important book. It's the magical and inescapable connection between consistent, disciplined execution and the freedom most of us truly seek in our businesses. Virginia Woolf said it best when she declared, "To enjoy freedom, we have to control ourselves." To many successful leaders, that seems counterintuitive. But as I've discovered, and as the hundreds of thousands of entrepreneurs we've helped have proven, it's absolutely true.

Another important discovery influenced my thinking about EOS in the early days, and it's beautifully articulated in *Process!* Very simply, running an entrepreneurial company is way different than being an executive in a big corporation. If you own or run a small, rapidly growing business, you likely have an almost-full-time job "in the trenches." One minute you may find yourself talking with a customer; the next, you're fixing a machine on the shop floor. Next, you're meeting with your banker, spending a few minutes picking up cigarette butts outside the loading dock, and then interviewing a new machine operator. Somewhere in there, you've got to find time to think, solve problems, lead and manage people, etc. It may be interesting, but it can be exhausting.

In contrast, successful leaders spend nearly *all* their time thinking strategically, building important relationships, making important decisions, and leading others. In short, rather than working *in* the business, they spend time working *on* the business and, ultimately, bring greater value to the company. Though it may seem obvious today, at the time I was developing EOS it was almost revolutionary to believe that the tools we needed as entrepreneurial leaders should be different, too.

Building on this important discovery, *Process!* carefully lays out an approach for consistent and disciplined execution that can be led by the busy people who run entrepreneurial companies. It's simple, high level, and practical—no theory, no wasted time or energy. Because it's simple and effective, it'll be more readily understood and adopted by people at every level of your organization. In other words, it'll take less time and make more of an impact than you might expect. Notably, it'll also work really well in a large corporation that wants to get a bigger bang for its buck than more complex business process improvement initiatives can deliver.

In a nutshell, this book is all about developing the ability to see your business through the lens of the core processes that comprise your business, and then making sure every core process is right and followed by everyone in your organization with absolute consistency. As a result, you'll create peace of mind, more consistency, scalability, ease of management, and more profit. In addition, you'll greatly increase the value of your company.

As Paton and Lisa mention in this book, five of my clients have sold to large billion-dollar companies at very high multiples. In each of these cases, the acquiring company described them as "one of the best-run companies we've ever considered acquiring." This was largely due to my clients' applying every word contained in this book.

That's the kind of impact reading this book and implementing what it teaches could have on your business (and, more importantly, your life). So please, read on, and put the principles Paton and Lisa share to work for you. I've spent my whole business life wanting to have a huge, positive impact on the world and, at the same time, be truly free. If that's what you want, too, *Process!* can make it happen.

—Gino Wickman, *Founder, EOS Worldwide*

COMMIT

CHAPTER 1

THE RIGHT MINDSET

Magic occurs when you blend a culture of
discipline with an ethic of entrepreneurship.
—Jim Collins

Nearly every entrepreneurial story begins with passion—for an innovative idea, a useful skill, a way to build a better mousetrap or make the world a better place. In the early days, this passion fuels the company's founder and gives its people real purpose, positive energy, and a vibrant culture. That passion helps a small, growing company attract and keep top talent, generate attention in the marketplace, and take business away from more well-established competitors.

For business leaders, this initial stage of energizing growth and unlimited possibility feels like magic. Imagine Henry Ford when his dream came true and the first Model T rolled off the assembly line in 1908. Think of how Sara Blakely felt when Spanx generated $4 million in revenue in its first year (all while she was still working full-time selling fax machines). Those epic moments are fueled by great ideas, unbridled optimism, and real passion.

Belief and enthusiasm aren't the only fuels necessary in a growing company, however. As former US Secretary of State General Colin Powell said, "A dream doesn't become reality through magic; it takes sweat, determination, and hard work." Every growing organization ultimately reaches a point where passion is simply not enough. The founder and leaders begin to realize that "what got us here won't get us there." Here's how it typically plays out:

A founder starts a business on her own and enjoys some early success. As demand increases, she spends increasing amounts of time "*in* the business—selling, serving customers, doing the books, sweeping the shop floor, and so on. There's precious little time for the things she's passionate about—creating, promoting, problem-solving, thinking strategically, and building important relationships. She tries to fix the problem by hiring her first employee, only to realize that hiring, training, and managing even one high-quality person is *a lot* of work. Hiring more people actually seems to *increase* the amount of time she spends on the things she doesn't enjoy. She becomes stuck and frustrated, and that early-stage passion begins to wane.

We call this "hitting the ceiling." As Larry E Greiner's *Harvard Business Review* article "Evolution and Revolution as Organizations Grow" proved, hitting the ceiling is inevitable for all growth-minded companies. So leaders who want to build great companies need to get really good at anticipating and breaking through these ceilings. Those who don't will see their organizations flatline or flame out.

More than 80 percent of businesses fail in their first five years, and only about 10 percent survive beyond year ten. Even for those that do survive, their owners and leaders often feel overwhelmed, frustrated, and unable to live the lives they want.

The good news is that you don't have to be one of those statistics. We know first-hand that it is *not* your lot in life to fail or feel miserable at work and bring those problems home every night. We've helped thousands of leaders just like you get themselves (and their teams) unstuck. This book captures those lessons. Like every book in the *Traction Library*, it is designed to help you understand why you're stuck and give you the specific tools to get consistently better results and reclaim your life.

We present a simple and proven solution to a problem faced by nearly all fast-growing companies: *inconsistent execution*. There's no theory in what we're about to share, just a set of timeless principles and practical tools that will help you break through the ceiling, run a better business, and live a better life. All we need from you is an open mind and a willingness to embrace what we're teaching.

That may seem like a simple request, but some find it surprisingly difficult.

Because no matter how frustrating and painful it is to be stuck, far too many leaders dismiss the type of important change we describe in this book as uninteresting, unnecessary, or even scary. Sadly, they're rejecting the very thing they need most—like an infant spitting out medicine or a drowning man fighting off a lifeguard.

That "thing" is *process*.

For too many leaders the mere mention of the dreaded "P word" invokes yawns, eye rolls, anxiously checked watches, and hasty exits. Entrepreneurs, innovators, and creative leaders want to be free—and our perception of process is not at all aligned with our thirst for freedom. We're energized by big-picture thinking, building an amazing culture, solving impossible problems, and growing something from nothing. Procedures, details, and rules—not so much.

And therein lies the paradox of process.

Because to be truly free as the owner or leader of a growing business, you must commit to a level of rigor, discipline, and consistency that may seem contrary to the way you're hardwired. To get everything you want from your business and create the freedom to live the life you once dreamed was possible, you must embrace process, not reject it.

To be fair, some leaders do. They're obsessed about figuring out the right and best way to do things and work hard to instill rigor and discipline for consistent execution. Others may know this work is important but lack the tools or the time to make it happen. If you're already a believer, great! This content will help you get others on your team as excited about process as you are, and lay out a simple, efficient way to unlock the power of process. If you're still skeptical, please keep reading. The stronger your aversion to instilling rigor and discipline for process, the more opportunity you have to find value in what follows. We intend to prove that getting a handful of core processes documented, simplified, and followed by all will *create* freedom, not destroy it.

To do that, we'll draw from the simple concepts and practical tools created by Gino Wickman, creator of the Entrepreneurial Operating System (EOS). EOS works to strengthen an organization's "Six Key Components": Vision, People, Data, Issues, Process, and Traction. This book provides a deep dive into the EOS way of strengthening your company's Process Component, while *increasing* your capacity for big picture thinking, innovation, and growth. There's no need to be an EOS expert to get value from this book, but those who'd like to learn more will find a brief overview on page 21, as well as at EOSworldwide.com. Rest assured, however. Even readers unfamiliar with EOS will understand and benefit from the approach and tools described in the pages that follow.

In the spirit of practicing what we preach, we'll start by describing what you're about to learn and implement using a simple illustration. We call it "The *Process!* Process."

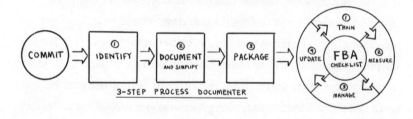

Section I will help you *Commit* fully to the journey ahead. With the proper mindset, you will fully appreciate the positive impact that strengthening your Process Component can have on your business and your life. In section II, you will *Learn* exactly how to make that happen in your organization by using two EOS Tools, the 3-Step Process Documenter and the FBA Checklist. Finally, section III, *Act* will provide you with the step-by-step process, templates, and resources to craft and implement a custom action plan for your organization.

So, let's get started. To gain your full commitment to this work, we'll first explore three common causes of anti-process bias in the minds of entrepreneurial leaders. While understandable and often deeply held, these beliefs are rooted in faulty logic. They are myths—pure and simple—and we hope to help you let them go.

MYTH 1: PROCESS IS NOT IN MY NATURE

Most successful entrepreneurs and innovative leaders are rugged individu-
alists. They're creators, disruptors,
and challengers of the *status quo*.
As a result, the very idea of doing
something the same way over and
over again seems intolerable. But
that's not what *process oriented* really
means. When we examine the subject
more thoroughly, it becomes clear that
all humans—even the most innovative—are
naturally and instinctively process oriented.

To take a much larger view, the very survival of the human species can be credited to adaptive process orientation. Our ancestors
learned to stop doing deadly things (like eating poisonous berries)
and continue doing what kept them alive (like sleeping together in
protected shelters). They shared that acquired knowledge with the
next generations through storytelling, cave paintings, and more.
As they learned new techniques for survival and perpetuating the
species—like creating fire and making tools—those improvements
were shared with others. They were gradually woven into the way a
family or a tribe operated. Those that mastered these new, improved
processes lived safer, less stress-
ful, and longer lives. We've been
incorporating successful habits
into our lives and discarding
the dangerous ones from our
daily habits for millennia.

This is also the way most successful businesses are built from the ground up. The founder decides to build a product or deliver a service, starts telling people about it, and generates a lead. Soon he's won his first customer and starts delivering. At this stage, he's likely relying on equal parts talent, passion, grit, and abject fear. Every time he delivers something that makes the customer smile, he thinks, *I'll keep doing that.* If the customer frowns, he concludes, *I'll never do* that *again.* Over time and through trial and error, he improves the way he builds the product or delivers the service. Soon he's seeing a ton of smiles and very few frowns.

Without really thinking about it, he's developing a repeatable way of delivering value to his customers. Instinctively, this way of operating becomes automatic. Nothing is written down. There are no manuals, workflow diagrams, or training guides. He's just learned what works best and repeats it consistently because it takes less time, feels better, and gets results. Whenever he sees opportunities to simplify or improve something, he seamlessly weaves a change into what has become a natural, consistent business process.

This instinctive feel and relentless drive for consistent execution and continuous improvement may not feel like being process oriented to you. But that's *exactly* what it is. It's not about creating mountains of standard operating procedures (SOPs) and inflexible compliance cultures. It's the innate gift all entrepreneurs have for observing what works best, replicating it, then learning and improving over time.

You don't reject process because you are *not* naturally process oriented. You reject it because you *are*. As a successful human and entrepreneur, you've been applying discipline for process throughout your life, without conscious thought. You didn't stop to think through how best to do things—there wasn't any time (or money) for that. You didn't *consciously* document anything or stop to pass on what you learned along the way—there was nobody else to teach or train! By the time you hired your first few employees, much of what you learned through trial and error probably seemed obvious to your now well-trained eye.

Yet, the actions that create consistently exceptional results are not at all obvious to most people in a growing business. Letting employees figure it out for themselves is inefficient and costly. Whether you've hired one person or forty people, nobody else has seen what you've seen and learned what you learned. Our approach will help you efficiently share the gift of your personal and organizational experience with every single member of your team. That will benefit you, your business, your team members, and everyone your organization serves.

We acknowledge how hard it can be to embrace something that never seemed necessary while you were building a successful business from scratch. We appreciate your concern that cumbersome rules or rigid guidelines might destroy the value you've created without process. But we also know that investing the time to stop, observe what's happening, settle on an optimal way to do something, write it down, teach it to others, and then measure and manage people until they get it right is *worth it*. It'll make your business better, get you out of the weeds, and allow you to live a better life.

So please, embrace the belief that process *is* in your nature. It has already played an important (if subconscious) role in helping you build your business. We will show you, step-by-step, how to do it efficiently and comfortably—by documenting and simplifying what you've learned, and then getting those core processes followed by all. Heck, you may even enjoy the journey.

MYTH 2: PROCESS TAKES TOO MUCH TIME

In all our years helping leaders, we've yet to hear a single person complain about having *too much* free time. The ability to do amazing things with very little time, money, or people—an almost superhuman resourcefulness—is a common and essential trait in successful early-stage companies. As with most blessings, though, it can also be a  curse. It can create the mistaken belief that being overwhelmed is acceptable, that you're *supposed to* feel like "the hurried-er I go, the behind-er I get."

Accepting that mindset as a permanent condition of all busy leaders is inaccurate and dangerous. Yes, great leaders can push through *brief* periods of overwhelming stress. They can write the code, fix the bugs, secure the clients, push out the software updates, answer emails, deposit checks, pay the bills, and start all over again. Day after day after day—to a point. For even the heartiest of leaders, however, bad stuff starts happening at work (and at home) after six to nine months of feeling like there's never enough time. If you're one of those leaders who feels you must choose between your personal wellness and health of your business you are not alone. That is a choice nobody should have to make.

> If you don't have time to do it right, when
> will you have time to do it over?
> **—John Wooden**

UCLA's legendary basketball coach reminds us that doing things right the first time will help us all stop trying to cram twenty pounds of manure in a ten-pound bag. In his career at UCLA, Wooden won ten NCAA national men's basketball championships in a twelve-year period, including a record seven in a row. His teams still hold the record for winning eighty-eight consecutive games.

He was a firm believer in the power of process. Many of his former players love sharing the famous story of the first team meeting each season. New players—nearly all of them heralded recruits—showed up expecting a rousing speech, an intense strategy session, or a grueling workout. Instead, Wooden spent *the entire meeting* on a step-by-step demonstration of how to properly put on socks. Yes, socks.

Why? In Wooden's day, basketball shoes weren't great. Blisters were a common problem that could knock valued players out of games. So, even though he was busy with the demands of building a basketball dynasty, the coach invested time personally teaching a basic, redundant action to his new superstars. The value of this lesson extended well beyond blister reduction. From day one, every member of the team knew that the UCLA Bruins do the "little things" right the first time, every time.

This story illuminates two flaws in the takes-too-much-time argument. Entrepreneurs *underestimate* how much time is wasted by their inattention to process. They also *overestimate* the time it will take to invest in strengthening their organization's Process Component.

First, entrepreneurs may underestimate the cumulative time their team spends addressing the needs of an unhappy customer, rebuilding a product, or repeating a service. Defective products, late shipments, and poor service experiences are costly mistakes that can turn your most important business partner into a former customer who's bad-mouthing you in the market. Recovering from these mistakes takes time. Frequent delays, errors, and inconsistencies can stymie growth and turn a healthy profit into a devastating loss, which few small businesses can survive.

Entrepreneurs may also underestimate the time wasted inside their organizations as a result of employee turnover caused by lack of process. When a valuable team-member quits, processing the termination, re-posting the job, and hiring and onboarding their replacement is time consuming and expensive. But it's more than that. High turnover erodes culture, which means leaders and managers have to spend more time on damage control and rebuilding that culture. When teams are shorthanded, supervisors, managers, and leaders get pulled away from their own jobs into the weeds of the business. As a result, not only are your most expensive people doing their subordinate's work, they're also not able to do the jobs they are being paid to do. Furthermore, turnover is costly because one or more disgruntled employees airing their grievances on social media can damage your ability to attract and retain great people in a brutal labor market.

Investing in process pays huge financial, cultural, and emotional dividends right away. Your customers will get what they want, when they want it, at a fair price. Their word of mouth will help build your reputation in the market rather than damaging it. Your employees will be better at their jobs from the start, feel better about being part of your team, and stay longer. Your leaders and managers will more consistently hit numbers, complete priorities, and have time to improve, create, and innovate. So please, don't underestimate the value of this work.

It is also common to overestimate the time it takes to instill discipline for process in your business. This is understandable if you mistakenly believe it's necessary to document 100 percent of the steps in 100 percent of your processes to get 100 percent compliance from every employee. We call that the "100/100/100 approach," and it can be both overwhelming and ineffective. Even so, it's often the approach taken by large organizations, government agencies, or heavily regulated businesses. Heck, we were guilty of this ourselves. In preparation for a new hire, one of us vividly remembers spending a weekend attempting to document every step of a receptionist's job—starting with how to turn on the computer. The result was a beautiful, accurate but completely ignored "masterpiece" that sat in a binder collecting dust for years.

To be clear, we agree that business-process improvement initiatives like LEAN, Six Sigma, ISO, and BPM—to name a few approaches—have been materially improving businesses for decades. We know that certain industries even require these types of certifications to remain in compliance or maintain competitive standing.

For most entrepreneurial companies and high-performance teams, however, the level of detail required to complete these projects seems overwhelming and unnecessary. Often the faulty assumption that this important work will take more time than it really needs to, is the very reason it doesn't get done at all.

That's why our simple and useful 20/80 approach—using in-house knowledge and familiar terms and tools—wins the day for most entrepreneurial companies. It applies the logic of the Pareto Principle: If doing 20 percent of the work produces 80 percent of the results, why don't we start *there*? It takes far less time to get started, the work product is more useful today, and more easily updated over time. If you need to be more detailed, start with our high-level approach, make an immediate impact, and build from there. But please get started!

Erik Piasio, the president of American Surgical Company (a medical device manufacturer that makes small sponges for use in spine and brain surgeries) explains the value of this approach. "For eight or nine years we had relied heavily on lean manufacturing methods and we were deep into Six Sigma, as well," he explained. "It had a positive impact, but we got lost in the weeds. It felt as though we were going overboard. EOS's 20/80 approach helped everyone—from people making $16 an hour to folks making $100,000 a year—understand and apply these tools to get consistently better results."

Yes, strengthening your Process Component will take some time. It doesn't need to take anywhere near as much time as you think it will. It will also save you far more time than you know. So please, follow Coach Wooden's lead and reject the myth that documenting, simplifying, and getting your core processes followed by all will take too much time.

MYTH 3: PROCESS DESTROYS FREEDOM

If you believe that instilling discipline for process means you and your people can no longer be creative, flexible, or innovative, you are not alone. This mistaken belief may be more widely held and fiercely defended than the first two. Even notable entrepreneurs like Elon Musk have expressed this fear, stating:

I don't believe in process. At a lot of big companies, process becomes a substitute for thinking. You're encouraged to behave like a little gear in a complex machine. It allows you to keep people who aren't that smart, aren't that creative.

It is true that many organizations overemphasize complying with detailed and inflexible processes. That approach leaves the most capable and creative employees feeling undervalued, as Jim Collins describes in *Good to Great*:

The purpose of bureaucracy is to compensate for incompetence and lack of discipline. Most companies build their bureaucratic rules to manage the small percentage of wrong people on the bus, which in turn drives away the right people, which then increases the percentage of wrong people, which increases the need for more bureaucracy to compensate for incompetence and lack of discipline, which then further drives the right people away, and so forth.

Yuck. No capable leader wants to be part of an organization stuck in a vicious cycle like that. However, what these two business thought leaders are describing is process run amok. It's an extreme, unnecessary, and ineffective approach, and it's *not at all* what this book is about.

Rejecting the idea of strengthening your Process Component for this reason is falling prey to a *false dichotomy*, a logical exercise used by debaters and con artists to convince people that only two options exist. It's like one of your kids saying, "Either you buy me this new video game, or you don't love me." It's a flawed argument for three reasons.

First, growing a strong, sustainable company *requires* consistent execution, no matter how creative you are. Take Bruce Springsteen. He is a uniquely original musician and a fierce advocate of freedom. He's also been a superstar for forty years in a notoriously fickle business. He attributes that success to consistent execution. "Getting an audience is hard," he explains. "Sustaining an audience is hard. It demands a consistency of thought, of purpose, and of action over a long period of time."

In other words, creativity and freedom alone might make you a one-hit wonder, but it won't help you build a business that stands the test of time. The good news is that building a business which is both disciplined *and* free is not only possible, it is quite common. Many successful companies have proven that getting important things done well every time does not require the bureaucratic nightmares anti-process pundits decry.

Collins finishes his thought from above by explaining exactly how rapidly growing companies execute consistently without creating unnecessary bureaucracy. They do it by establishing a *culture of discipline*, which he defines as "disciplined people who engage in disciplined thought and take disciplined action—operating with freedom within a framework of responsibilities—this is the cornerstone of a culture that creates greatness."

Applying the tools in this book will help you create such a culture. It will help you quickly construct a clear, simple, high-level framework of responsibilities within which smart, creative people can operate freely and consistently achieve objectives.

The second flaw in this argument? What's *really* robbing leaders of the freedom they seek isn't *too much* process—it's a *lack* of process. We know this because entrepreneurs often ask for our help at the very moment they're feeling like captives of the business they created. Many describe it as being stuck *in* the business, with no time to think and work *on* the business—where their vision, passion, and creativity can really make a difference.

In a business where everybody does things their own way, leaders inevitably get stuck in the day-to-day. They spend more time answering and re-answering basic questions, redirecting people, and fixing problems caused by reinventing ways to do work that should be routine. Our approach to process will break that cycle simply and efficiently. It will help your team master the basics in a way that gets consistently better results day-to-day. That will, in turn, help you and your team spend less time in the trenches and *more* time thinking, creating, and innovating.

Isadore Sharp, founder of Four Seasons Hotels and Resorts, leveraged this common-sense approach to do what he called "systemizing the predictable, so you can humanize the exceptional." He encouraged leaders, managers, and team members to systemize basic routines, such as checking in a guest at the front desk or cleaning a hotel room. He hired talented, service-minded people and trained them to master these important, repeatable actions. Finally, he and his fellow leaders encouraged team members to use their own judgment and discretion to create truly memorable experiences. Guests joyfully share stories of team members remembering their names and drink orders, providing warm hats, mittens, and robes for their children on a surprisingly cold day, or hand delivering a book from a favorite author. As a result, Sharp and his team built Four Seasons into one of the world's top luxury hotel chains—known for exceptional customer service and attention to detail.

That's what using this simple and practical approach will help you and your team do. It also underscores the final flaw in the argument that "discipline for process" and "mountains of red tape" are synonymous. Far from creating a dystopian bureaucracy full of mindless robots, leveraging this approach will help you systemize the predictable and spend more time humanizing the exceptional.

Process doesn't destroy freedom; process *creates* freedom.

THE POWER OF BELIEF

Rejecting these myths and any anti-process bias you may have is a vital first step. For this journey to be successful, however, you must do more than suspend your active resistance to process. We need you to truly believe in the power of this work and support this effort fully.

> When you believe in something, the force of your
> convictions will spark other people's interest and
> motivate them to help you achieve your goals.
> **—Sir Richard Branson**

As a successful entrepreneur, author, and founder of the Virgin Business Group, Branson helps us understand that when leaders are "all in," their people will be too. If you don't believe in the power of process with the full force of your convictions, your people won't either. They'll view this as another flavor-of-the-month initiative, bide their time until you become bored with it, and revert to old habits as soon as they're able. Your apathy, abdication, or half-hearted support won't help you get better results, live a better life, or achieve your company's vision.

If you want things to change, what needs to change first is *you*. Only when you overcome your own anti-process bias will you be able to help others overcome theirs. Show your people the genuine enthusiasm that you instinctively have for getting important things done consistently well. Participate alongside your team in the discussions, debates, and work that needs to be done to strengthen your Process Component. Your passion, years of experience, and accumulated wisdom are invaluable on this journey; share them freely.

With your belief and genuine support, what you and your team are about to learn will pay enormous dividends. Your business will run more smoothly, achieve better results, and increase in value. You'll have more time for important stuff at work and at home. Your peace of mind will improve, and you'll have more fun.

Yes, it may require sweat, determination, and hard work. It may not be magic, but it's absolutely worth it. Process *will* set you free.

CHAPTER 2

. . . .

WHY IS PROCESS IMPORTANT?

Process. *noun:* pro·cess | \ ˈprä-ˌses, ˈprō-, -səs \
a set of actions or operations that achieves a desired result.

Why write an entire book about process?

In our experience, process has not yet been explained and taught in a way that inspires entrepreneurs and other innovative, growth-oriented leaders to embrace it. Too many driven, hard-working business owners and leaders do not get the results they want and are not living their ideal lives. If you're one of them, our simple approach to documenting and simplifying core processes will help.

Think back to when you launched your business, joined your team, or were selected as a leader. What excited you most? What did you believe was possible? It could have been anything: building a better mousetrap, delivering amazing service to customers, creating a culture that attracts and enriches great people, or building something of enduring value and achieving economic freedom. Whatever that was, it's all still possible.

If your business doesn't consistently generate the desired results, instilling discipline for process will—by definition—be the key to making that happen. This chapter is all about understanding *why* process will make a powerful difference for your business and your life. First, we will *define* what we mean by a "strong Process Component." We'll then illustrate the many *benefits* of doing this work. Finally, we'll alert you to the *costs* of an inattention to process.

WHAT IS A STRONG PROCESS COMPONENT?

Before we teach you how to instill more discipline for process in your business, it might be helpful to understand what a strong Process Component looks like in the context of a company running on EOS. For those not familiar with the Entrepreneurial Operating System (EOS), the summary on the next two pages will explain some of the terms and concepts we use in this book. If you're already familiar with EOS, this summary will be a helpful refresher.

More than ten thousand entrepreneurial companies have strengthened their Process Component by getting a handful of core processes "documented, simplified, and followed by all." When that happens, every one of your people will know how to do the most important things the right and best way. This doesn't mean nobody ever makes a mistake or skips a step, but it *does* mean that you're consistently getting the results you want. When mistakes or delays inevitably occur, your team members will know about it and be accountable for fixing it and getting better the next time.

AN EOS OVERVIEW

EOS is a simple way of operating a business. It's a complete system, full of timeless concepts and simple, practical tools that help owners and leaders get what they want from their businesses. Through painstaking study and years of trial and error, Gino Wickman discovered how to help leadership teams resolve the hundreds of common issues facing an entrepreneurial company.

What Gino found was that each and every common issue was caused by weakness in Vision, People, Data, Issues, Process, or Traction—what we call the Six Key Components of any business—as illustrated in the EOS Model.

Whether implementing the EOS Tools and concepts on their own or with the aid of an EOS Implementer, leadership teams follow a Proven Process (as you might imagine) to strengthen each of these Six Key Components.

THE EOS MODEL

VISION · DATA · PROCESS · TRACTION · ISSUES · PEOPLE · YOUR BUSINESS

A strong **Vision** Component means everyone in the organization is 100 percent on the same page with where the company is going and exactly how it plans to get there. A strong **People** Component means you've clearly defined what a "great person" means in your unique organization, and you're great at attracting and retaining them. A strong **Data** Component means you're running your business on a handful of numbers that give you an absolute pulse on your business, predict future results, and help you make better, faster decisions.

A company with a strong **Issues** Component can solve issues as they arise and make them go away forever—rather than letting them linger for weeks, months, and sometimes even years. A strong **Process** Component, of course, is about getting the most important things in your business done the right and best way every time. And finally, a strong **Traction** Component is about instilling discipline and accountability at all levels of the organization so that, everywhere you look, everyone is executing on your vision day in and day out.

The journey to implement EOS is a journey to strengthen *all* Six Key Components. Many leaders mistakenly believe that they can solve all the issues in their business by just working on one or two of them, but we know from experience that becoming 80 percent strong or better in each of the Six Key Components will help you run a truly great business. To get a clear picture of your organizational strength in each of the Six Key Components, visit organizationalcheckup.com.

Building such a well-oiled machine is not a new concept. Business thought leaders such as W. Edwards Deming, Peter Drucker, Phil Crosby, Tom Peters, and many more have created or shared many acronym-infused ways to make it happen, including business-process improvement (BPI), business process management (BPM), management by objectives (MBO), and continuous improvement (CI). Many business leaders are familiar with the LEAN or Six Sigma approaches to improving quality and consistency. Masaaki Imai, the renowned organizational theorist and management consultant, described it as *kaizen*, loosely translated from Japanese as "change for the better."

The accessible approach in this book consolidates and simplifies many of these concepts to ensure that you, your people, and your business are always changing for the better. In his book *The E-Myth Revisited*, Michael E. Gerber captured the essence of these concepts, calling it the "Franchise Prototype":

> *A proprietary way of doing business that successfully and preferentially differentiates every extraordinary business from every one of its competitors.*

A strong Process Component builds a high-level blueprint for executing consistently well today *and* improving and innovating as required. Investing time in this simple discipline will yield extraordinary results and help your business outperform the competition. The story on the next few pages is an example of how a clear, unwavering vision and discipline for process helped one family build a fast-food business with a devoted and loyal following.

STRONG VISION, STRONG PROCESS, STRONG BUSINESS

In 1948, Harry and Esther Snyder founded the beloved hamburger chain In-N-Out Burger. It is still family owned and operated today. The first drive-thru hamburger restaurant in Southern California was built on the premise that hamburgers could be done differently. From the start, the Snyders believed in serving food that was never frozen, never under heat lamps, and never microwaved. They've always believed in hiring great people and taking good care of them. They've always wanted to delight their customers and keep them coming back.

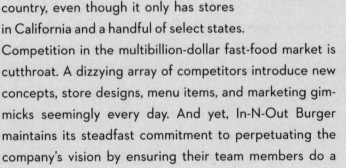

The founders' clear vision and the company's consistent execution of those founding principles has resulted in a cult-like following throughout the country, even though it only has stores in California and a handful of select states. Competition in the multibillion-dollar fast-food market is cutthroat. A dizzying array of competitors introduce new concepts, store designs, menu items, and marketing gimmicks seemingly every day. And yet, In-N-Out Burger maintains its steadfast commitment to perpetuating the company's vision by ensuring their team members do a handful of things really well, every time.

If you've ever been to an In-N-Out Burger, you'll see an impressively well-oiled machine. Everything they do at the corporate and store level is aligned with the company's principles and consistently followed. Their menu is relentlessly simple—hamburgers, french fries, and drinks. They take orders and then prepare and serve meals using a series of simple, predictable steps. As a result, they're able to quickly train new employees on food preparation, move customers through very busy stores at a remarkable rate, and deliver memorable service to their customers.

In-N-Out Burger also has a disciplined and documented process for selecting new locations. Of course, they consider population, demographics, traffic, and other factors that drive success. Specifically, however, their process requires that each new restaurant is built within three hundred miles of a company-owned distribution center to enable the regular delivery of fresh and high-quality ingredients.

Getting team members and almost three hundred franchisees to follow these core processes has helped In-N-Out consistently outperform the competition. Their stores are almost always surrounded by long lines of cars, and their lobbies are filled with happy customers, lined up for fresh food, big smiles, and a consistently exceptional experience. The company generates more than $1 billion per year in annual revenue and is debt free. In comparison, their sales beat an average McDonald's by almost double with a profit margin estimated to be 20 percent higher than their rivals and other restaurant chains.

The dividends of their commitment to process continue. They often win best-places-to-work awards, and their team members enjoy higher than average salaries, paid vacations, and the right to participate in the company's 401(k) plan. Their employee turnover rate is at least 75 percent lower than the industry average, and a store manager's average tenure is *seventeen years*. No matter how you judge exceptional performance—financial results, beating the competition, delighting customers, or attracting and retaining top talent—In-N-Out Burger has proven that rigor and discipline for process can help you get everything you want from your business.

THE BENEFITS OF A STRONG PROCESS COMPONENT

It's easy to forget that every large, successful company began as a small, entrepreneurial business. Companies like In-N-Out Burger made the leap successfully because they were committed to consistent execution long before they became a billion-dollar company. They spent time figuring out what truly mattered, weaved that into clear, simple guidelines for execution, and helped team members follow those processes. In other words, to scale your business and achieve your vision, you must start instilling discipline and accountability now, while you're still a small, growing company.

The good news is the tools we're sharing were created specifically for privately-held entrepreneurial companies with between 10 and 250 employees. Their owners and leaders are growth-oriented, open-minded, and driven by a desire to build something of enduring value while serving their customers and employees well. These businesses include manufacturers, distributors, professional service firms, tech companies, retailers—you name it. No matter the type, industry, or size of your business, strengthening your Process Component will yield specific benefits:

1. **You'll grow faster** (and more sustainably). When your marketing and sales processes are documented, simplified, and followed by all, you'll create more leads and increase your  win rate. You'll invest less time and money on unproductive or improperly-focused salespeople, or on marketing activities that don't produce results. Not only will you get better at acquiring new customers, but your discipline for process will help you retain and grow existing relationships as well. Moreover, many of the leaders we spoke with for this book agreed that process is the key to removing themselves as the bottleneck (or "walking SOP") holding back the company's growth.

   Natalie Standridge was inspired to found Casa de Corazón when she couldn't find high-quality, dual-language childcare in her area. She and her dedicated team filled the void by providing care focused on environmental consciousness, intercultural learning, healthy diets, and Spanish-immersion curriculum for non-Spanish speakers. As demand grew rapidly,

Natalie knew she had to ensure every member of the Casa team would be able to meet the very high standards she had set and parents had come to expect.

Unable to be "in all places at all times," she documented and simplified her core processes and worked to get them followed by all. Today, Casa has produced more than 650 graduates and opened six locations. They have laid the groundwork to expand nationally, with each location capable of delivering consistently high-quality care and exceptional experiences for children and their parents.

Another entrepreneur was very candid with us about his early disdain for process at a rapidly growing collision center. He and his team knew their stuff, worked hard, and brought a "whatever-it-takes" mentality to every new location. They were kicking butt and taking names, so they felt strongly they didn't need process—until they clearly did.

One day the owner observed a simple question about a customer's invoice bring one location to a halt for over 15 minutes. Because each location and each employee had a unique way of doing things, getting a simple question answered required the input of all three employees involved in this one repair. The owner suddenly realized that similar debates were occurring daily at every location, involving sales orders, parts, repair processes, and lots of other stuff. Thankfully, his team responded quickly to eliminate this bottleneck and others like it. By documenting a handful of core processes and getting them followed consistently, the company kept growing.

2. **You'll attract and keep better talent.** As we write this book, finding and keeping great people is the number one problem

faced by growing businesses around the world. Strengthening your people (or talent, or HR) process will help your company get better at sourcing, recruiting, interviewing, hiring, onboarding, training, and supporting your employees.

One technology services company running on EOS solved this problem many years ago with innovative thinking, a willingness to change, and a new process. Hiring great people with specific experience was difficult. Because these talented people were scarce, retaining them was even more difficult. The company's Integrator shares a story about a new technical architect they hired at a very high salary, only to see him recruited away several weeks later at an annual salary that was $22,000 higher!

After trying every traditional way to solve this problem, the company's leadership team decided to stop competing for experienced talent and grow their own instead. This required a wholesale change to nearly every step in their people process.

They partnered with local technical schools and colleges to offer internships and cross-discipline training programs for passionate, talented students *before* they had selected a specific career path. They leased another floor in their office building and built a world-class technical training center. It took two years, but today the company is winning the talent war. They're attracting better people who share their company's core values. They're able to promote from within far more frequently than before making this change. Turnover is almost nonexistent. Their culture is vibrant, collaborative, and fun.

We've seen other clients vastly improve their ability to attract and retain great people with a people process designed to "humanize the exceptional." One client celebrates an employee's first day with decorations, balloons, and an enthusiastic welcoming committee. At the same time, they deliver a gift basket and thank you note to the employee's family, expressing appreciation for the time and commitment their loved ones are giving to the organization. Similarly, a CPA firm sends a handwritten note to each employee's significant other during their busy season (along with a generous gift certificate to a favorite dining spot) to say thank you for enduring the long hours and time that their family member spends away from home.

Recruiting and retaining great people goes beyond your HR process. Having your other core processes followed by all will keep your people safer, reduce mistakes, and make them really good at their jobs a lot faster. People who master the fundamentals feel confident and valuable. A consistently followed process for leading, managing, and driving accountability will help, too. It will create a proven way for building and maintaining a great culture, gathering feedback to ensure everyone is engaged, and recognizing and rewarding exceptional performance.

As a result, team members will see their bosses as supportive coaches who can help them improve and advance, versus critical opponents waiting to catch them messing up. As a result, great people will want to stay (and recruit talented friends) while marginal performers will feel pressure to improve or exit.

3. **You'll engage everyone in a culture of excellence.** In many organizations, excellence feels less like an attainable goal and

more like a business buzzword used by managers in a half-hearted effort to increase productivity. If you've hired the right people, the folks on the front lines want to do their jobs well. Without a strong Process Component, they each learn their own ways to get things done. Then those experienced (but self-taught) team members are asked to train their newer peers, and so on. This may work for a while, but it should concern you. It's akin to betting the bright future of your business on a high-stakes game of telephone.

Atul Gawande, physician and renowned author of *The Checklist Manifesto*, notes that the failure to proactively document best practices creates inconsistencies that get "embedded in the system." This happens without leaders or employees understanding the origins, purposes, or impacts of these inconsistencies. As Casa de Corazón's Natalie Standridge shared, "Before we documented and simplified our core processes, people would reinvent the wheel. They did their best, but in many cases they wouldn't meet the standards that we created for our customers and children."

In contrast, a strong Process Component provides a clear baseline of simple, repeatable actions that produce desired results. Every employee sees the value of doing it the same way, no matter their level of experience. When processes are documented, a business can expect consistency of action, predictability of outcomes, and a foundation from which you can consistently improve each process. Rather than grappling with a culture of inconsistency, you'll have embedded a culture of excellence.

4. **Your customers will be happier.** What about the people or businesses that you serve? Core marketing and sales processes create a consistent set of realistic expectations in the marketplace. One or more core operations processes will help you consistently deliver high-quality products and great service.

Consistently meeting expectations will help you build a strong brand, delight your customers, and decrease the likelihood of their leaving for the competition.

Perhaps more importantly, a documented, simplified core process for customer satisfaction and loyalty will help you better understand the needs of each customer so you can consistently meet or exceed those needs, and proactively validate their loyalty with customer feedback surveys or regular business reviews. When you track customer satisfaction data, respond to constructive feedback, and show your customers how hard you're working to execute well and continuously improve, relationships are forged, and great things happen!

Many of our clients weave steps into their core processes designed to surprise and delight customers. A construction company running on EOS used an improved project-management process to do just that. Before documenting and simplifying that process, they would identify the client's needs, design and build the space, and close the project with little fanfare. The company's leaders noticed that many homeowners would celebrate the project's successful completion on their own—inviting neighbors, friends, and the construction company's team.

They decided to incorporate this excitement into their project process, adding a ribbon-cutting celebration to the project-closing step. Now, as a project nears completion, the company collects the homeowners' guest list, purchases the food and drinks, and often celebrates with the customer, neighbors, and friends. As a result, the customers are treated to a fun and unexpected celebration at the end of their project and the company regularly receives referrals.

Whether it's due to more consistent execution, wow experiences, or both—a strong Process Component means fewer customers will leave for the competition, the size and breadth of your relationships will increase, and you'll get free PR and more referrals from raving fans.

5. **You'll have more time.** As Coach Wooden reminded us, doing things right creates more time for everyone. Documented core processes help new employees get up to speed and begin contributing much faster. Managers deal with fewer basic questions and can spend their precious time coaching, mentoring, developing people, and improving processes. You and fellow leaders will have more time to imagine, think, strategize, plan, and (gasp!) lead.

An entrepreneur shared that when he and his family started their pest-control company, he insisted on a culture where employees could be creative and express themselves in their own unique ways. Being a free spirit himself, the owner didn't want to stymie anyone's freedom. As the months passed, however, the entire leadership team felt the burden that the absence of process was causing. They were overwhelmed with day-to-day management and unable to successfully train their teams or grow their company.

Channeling the passion that only an entrepreneur can generate, that very owner became a huge proponent of process. He came to realize documenting the company processes would improve results *and* give his team access to the freedom he'd been hoping for from the start. Today he plays a key role in designing the training for new and existing employees in operations. He and his fellow leaders spend more time sharing the company's vision and leading people, and far less time in the trenches.

The benefits of having more time extends well beyond the workplace, of course. Disciplined, consistent execution in the business will free up time for your own passions, family, and friends. And that pursuit is neither luxurious nor selfish. Busy leaders who also enjoy their personal lives and take time to recharge are *always* more effective and valuable than those who feel overwhelmed by the day-to-day. Even if the extra time is used to "do nothing," as author Anne LaMott said in *Bird by Bird*, "Almost everything will work again if you unplug it for a few minutes . . . including you."

6. **You'll get better at resolving issues.** Having an agreed-upon way of doing the important things in your business will help you more quickly and accurately determine *why* you're not getting the results you want. In contrast, a team that hasn't yet decided how to do the most important things consistently well often jumps to inaccurate conclusions about why the business isn't growing fast enough, or generating enough profit, or attracting and retaining enough great people, or serving its customers well.

Jason Smylie, owner and president of Capriotti's Sandwich Shop and Wing Zone, provides a great example of how clearly-defined processes make it easier to track down the root cause of an issue: "If our customer satisfaction score is below expectations, we backtrack to our processes to see where we can make an improvement. We run a report to see why the score is low. Or discuss it with our team. Or make a site visit. It's a standard approach when we're not performing as expected. We start by looking at our processes. What steps did we miss or fail to follow? Once that's clear, we train, measure, and manage to improve our results."

When it comes to resolving issues, sometimes a bad (or no) process can make good people look like bad people, as the story below illustrates.

PEOPLE OR PROCESS?

"One of them has to go," said Sheila, the company president. The owner and other members of the leadership team nodded in grim agreement. "Maybe both," said Michael, the head of operations. "We may have two 'wrong people.'"

Jen, the production manager, and Dave, the HR director, seemed to hate each other. Often when they worked together, they nearly came to blows.

"It happens every time we hire someone," Michael pointed out. "They argue about everything: How do we gather and evaluate resumes? Who makes the screening call? Who does the interview? How and when do we make the offer? Every time it's an ugly battle."

After separate meetings with each emotional leader, the president was left feeling stuck and exhausted. She called her EOS Implementer and said, "Can you help me figure out which one is worth saving?"

"What does the process say?" the EOS Implementer asked.

After a long silence, Sheila sheepishly answered, "What process?"

In the end, Sheila and the team realized the root cause of this clash of personalities was not unresolvable personal conflict, but the lack of a clear hiring step in their HR process. So they got to work documenting and simplifying it. The discussion was spirited. It produced several strong disagreements about critical steps, but they ultimately reached agreement about the way everybody should do it, not just Jen or Dave. As a result, both leaders remain on the team, and the company is doing a much better job of hiring and onboarding people.

7. **You'll make more money.** Now let's look at the bottom line. When your company is experiencing the benefits described above, your business will become more profitable. As a leader, you'll also be more valuable to the organization and compensated

appropriately for that value because you're able to spend less time in the day-to-day and more time leading.

The owners of a home service business experienced this benefit first-hand. Before strengthening their Process Component, the company endured years of high sales but low profits. Their facility operated in a subpar building and was so dirty that new employees were advised not to wear nice shoes because they would be ruined. People were working hard to serve the customers, but lacked the consistency and discipline to achieve their goals.

After acquiring the company from a family member, the new owner became frustrated with its disappointing results. "I didn't want to be that leader who expects everyone to do it his way," he said, "but we were stuck at the same revenue year after year. When we decided to document and follow a few core processes, we could see the results right away." Specifically, over two years the company saw revenue double (from $15M to $30M) and net profit jump from 3 percent to 10 percent. As results improved, so did the quality and cleanliness of the facilities, the morale and engagement of the employees, and the consistent level of service provided to the customers. Not only were the owners and the investors able to buy new shoes, but they could wear them in the shop too!

8. **Your company will become more valuable.** As the above story illustrates, investing in your Process Component can pay an exponential return. It's simple math—a $30M company with 10 percent profit, engaged employees, and loyal customers is *a lot* more valuable than a $15M company with 3 percent profit, higher turnover, and less repeat business.

Beyond that math, however, process can have an exponential impact on the value of your business. If you plan to share or transfer ownership someday—to a member of your family or leadership team, a private equity or venture capital firm, or a strategic buyer—a strong Process Component is essential. As *The E-Myth Revisited* author Michael E. Gerber said on the *Legal Mastermind* podcast, "If your business depends on people and not on process, your business does not have any value."

Gino Wickman, the creator of EOS who's been helping entrepreneurs maximize the value of their business and live better lives for more than twenty years, explains: "Five companies I worked with ultimately sold to billion-dollar corporations at very high multiples. In every case the purchaser indicated that these companies were the best-run businesses they had ever seen." One company sold to an outside investor for an unheard of multiple of more than *fifteen* times EBITDA—three times higher than average transactions in their space!

Put simply, what makes a business valuable is its ability to generate consistently excellent results without relying on the founder or a small group of experienced team members. If your business is valuable solely because you (and maybe others) are willing to work eighty hours a week, investors will be more likely to buy *you* or your best people than to pay a premium for the whole company. When a company is set up with the tools to run independent of its leaders, it is more valuable today—while you still own it—and, in the future, if you ever decide to sell some or all of it.

9. **You'll live a better life.** Yes, we realize that this is a bold claim. However, when you experience any specific one, if not all, of the benefits identified above—consistently attracting and retaining great people, growing faster, making customers happier, earning more money, and creating independent value—wouldn't your personal life improve as well?

    One of our clients grew tired of the exhaustion that accompanied the inconsistent performance of his business. The company enjoyed high sales and nationwide recognition, but it was not consistently profitable. Worse yet, doing the little things well (or cleaning up the mess when they weren't done well) seemed to require the owner's daily involvement. He was putting in countless hours working and worrying, traveling almost weekly to each location, and missing time at home with his young family.

    "In hindsight, my own resistance to process was the biggest hurdle to the company. Quite frankly, I don't like being told what to do, and I didn't think others would want to be told either. Ha! In fact, people would rather follow a process and win than figure it out on their own and flounder."

    The company implemented EOS and committed to strengthening the Process Component very early in their implementation journey. Today the founder's leadership team successfully and efficiently runs the business, leaving him with the opportunity to enjoy his sons' basketball games and his daughter's ski competitions. He and his family travel, sponsor (a dozen!) less fortunate children around the world through Compassion International, and live the life of their dreams.

    When your company is a well-oiled machine and no longer needs your day-to-day firefighting, you'll have the time, energy, and financial resources to pursue other passions. Countless successful business leaders contribute to causes beyond their business doors. For example, the owners and leaders at In-N-Out Burger created a foundation that gives 100 percent of the donations it receives to support abused children and to fund numerous philanthropic programs.

However you define your ideal life, a stronger Process Component will help free you up to live it. You deserve it.

THE COSTS OF A WEAK PROCESS COMPONENT

Not strengthening your Process Component can be expensive, risky, and even fatal to a growing organization. The most obvious costs are the inverse of those benefits listed above. A weak Process Component can stymie growth and erode profitability. You will have more trouble finding and keeping great people, and it will be harder to serve your customers well. That will make  your business more dependent on you, and, accordingly, less valuable. You'll have less time to lead *in* the business and little time to enjoy life *outside* of the business.

Here are three specific ways failing to strengthen your Process Component can harm your business:

1. **You will struggle to find and keep great people.** As noted above, without a proven approach for finding, recruiting, and

evaluating world-class candidates, winning the battle for the best people is nearly impossible.

Great people want to work for organizations that have a clear sense of who they are, where they're going, and how they plan to get there. They want to know exactly what's expected of them and feel confident that they can do the job well. They want a leader who cares enough to help them become successful and provides the necessary tools, training, resources, and feedback along the way.

Does your company have a carefully designed process for leading and managing its people? Are your team leaders, supervisors, and managers properly trained? Or are your employees at the mercy of the individual capabilities of each unique boss? Do you have clearly defined roles for each employee, and career paths for those who want to advance? Do you offer or encourage training and development? Do you reward and recognize top performers? The companies that are winning the talent war are doing all of these things consistently well.

Jason Smylie, the founder of Capriotti's and Wing Zone, mentioned earlier, was a self-described "Six Sigma process geek" in his life before fast-casual food service. He recalls discovering how valuable documented and simplified core processes could be in quickly and positively resolving people issues. In the early days, he and his partner struggled to retain people on his leadership and mid-management teams. These people were experienced and hard-working, but they just couldn't master the company's way of operating and generate consistently great results.

Once exposed to the 20/80 approach to strengthening the Process Component, Jason knew immediately he'd been missing a key ingredient in training and supporting great people. Quarter after quarter, one core process at a time, he and his team members aligned around the right way to do important things. The business began to grow and scale faster, and with a few exceptions, leaders and managers were able to grow and scale with it. Now when a leader is struggling, their issues can easily be traced back to a core process not being consistently followed. Most of the time Jason doesn't even need to get involved to resolve the issue, much less make a change on his leadership team.

The direct and indirect costs of poor engagement and retention are significant. The Gallup organization calls unnecessary turnover a fixable problem that costs US businesses $1 trillion per year. According to the Society for Human Resource Management (SHRM), companies spend between 50–75 percent of an employee's annual salary to recruit and train someone new. That means that replacing ten team members each year at an average salary of $60,000, would cost a business $300,000–$450,000 *annually!*

The indirect cost of turnover is even scarier. A business that's understaffed or full of new, inexperienced people is far less likely to meet growth goals, ship quality products on time, or deliver service that meets customer expectations. Everything—including your life—gets harder. You have more messes to clean up, more apologies to make, more overtime to pay, and more problems to solve. Talent experts Geoff Smart and Randy Street illustrate this point vividly in *Who: The A Method for Hiring*: "According to studies we've done with our clients the average hiring mistake costs fifteen times an employee's base salary in hard costs and productivity loss."

2. **Your business will stop growing.** Inconsistent execution in just about any area of your business can halt growth. For example, the lack of a solid marketing process leads many companies to spend a lot of time and money without building a strong brand, reaching the right prospects, differentiating themselves from the competition, or generating qualified leads. Without a great sales process, it's tough for companies to win new business consistently, build strong relationships, grow accounts over time, or get customer referrals. Without solid operations and finance processes, it is nearly impossible to keep those hard-earned customers happy beyond the sale or the business financially healthy. Here is an example of a company that suffered a drag on growth due to a lack of processes early on.

KNOW PROCESS, KNOW GROWTH

FBC Remodel (FBC) was growing quickly and profitably while effectively serving its customers in Colorado and Minnesota. Their locally run offices had received awards for their growth and were full of great people. They decided to add a third location, in Virginia, making them one of America's largest residential remodelers. Hopes were high, and out of the gate the location immediately set sales records.

Three short years later, however, the high hopes had been dashed, the location had been shut down, and FBC was scrambling to rebuild its reputation and its balance sheet. What happened? At every level, a lack of discipline for process.

In the company's first two locations, trusted and experienced managers made sure team members consistently followed carefully documented processes. They weren't perfect, but they were respected as important to the FBC way of operating. When somebody new didn't know what to do or how to do a task, the managers would redirect them to "follow the process."

In Virginia, however, the team was unaware of or disregarded those established post-sale processes. Instead, the leader and managers deferred to the work experience of its Virginia employees: "We failed to train the team on the processes that were proven successful," explained FBC's founder. "We thought that the people we hired were talented enough, and when they did it their way rather than ours, we allowed them too much leeway. This was the fatal mistake. By the time we realized the damage this was causing, it was too late."

To recover, the owners borrowed from personal accounts and invested an additional $500,000 to rebuild Virginia projects and leave the market. They refocused on serving their original markets and existing customers. Though expensive and humbling, those tough lessons eventually paid dividends. The team conducted a thorough postmortem, documenting what was learned and markedly increasing rigor and discipline for process.

Five years later the team followed their new-market process and opened a new location in Naperville, Illinois. They hired great people and painstakingly trained them on the company's core processes. They encouraged team members to use independent judgment within the framework of those processes, and it worked beautifully. Today, all three markets are thriving with happy customers and healthy balance sheets, and the organization has a scalable model for the future.

3. **Your business may fall behind or become obsolete.** Being strong in the Process Component means regularly reviewing, updating, and improving the way important things get done. Left unchecked, failing to observe long-held processes with a critical eye and make improvements as the world around you changes can put you out of business. That may sound overly dramatic, but it's precisely what happened to cab companies that had cornered the market in every major metro until two young entrepreneurs got an idea.

"THE WAY WE'VE ALWAYS DONE THINGS" CAN BE FATAL

For decades, taxis were the main source of business transportation in major metropolitan areas. The people who owned and ran traditional taxi companies seemed to have a distinct advantage—if not a near monopoly. A few dominant players and the government agencies regulating service standards and fares resulted in an industry that controlled who, how, when, and where business owners and cab drivers earned a living.

This old, tired business model had disastrous results. For consumers, hailing or ordering a cab varied from city to city and from company to company. Service levels were unpredictable at best and often disappointing. Earning a living as a cab driver was physically and financially risky and almost cost prohibitive. For example, in New York City, a taxi driver needed to buy their own medallion to become their own boss. In 2014, the price for that medallion was $1 million.

These antiquated customer-service and business-growth processes grew out of what Jim Collins calls the "hubris born of success." In his book *How the Mighty Fall*, Collins noted how industries go out of business when they view "success as an entitlement" or "lost sight of the underlying factors that created success in the first place." This hubris led to outdated processes for hiring, training, and compensating drivers, and serving customers. It also opened the door to disruption from outside the industry.

Enter Uber, whose founders were unhappy customers, not industry experts. Garrett Camp, a computer programmer, and his friend Travis Kalanick had trouble finding a taxi during a snowstorm. After spending $800 on a private driver and comparing notes on other disappointing experiences, they launched an early-stage version of the ride-sharing business. They built processes and used up-to-date technology to create a better experience.

While we appreciate that Uber's later practices are under scrutiny, Uber's process for finding, booking, and paying for a ride was instantly superior. The process to become a driver was simpler and less expensive. Their two-way rating system both rewarded excellent service and encouraged riders to behave well. All of these process innovations, driven by common sense and easy-to-use technology, changed the industry overnight.

After just three years of operating in only a handful of major markets, ride-sharing services like Uber and Lyft snatched away 8 percent of the business traveler market from rental car companies (55%) and taxis (37%). By 2018, they had grabbed 70.5 percent of the market, with rental cars getting 23.5 percent and taxis just 6 percent. Not coincidentally, in that same year, the cost of a New York City taxi medallion dropped by 80 percent to $180,000.

Whether limiting your ability to grow revenue, scale your business, or lose significant market share, these examples highlight the costs that a lack of process has on your business and life. Andre Durand founded Ping! Identity, an enterprise software solutions company that recently became publicly-traded. Durand explains how his growing organization was affected by these costs.

"In the early days, our growth was people dependent," he shared. "The sales knowledge we needed to grow existed in the head of one or two key people. Same with operations, customer service, accounting—you name it. If you compare our small business to a watch, at that point, the watch told the correct time, all the time.

"But when a company is dependent on people—not process—and tries to grow by adding products, services, locations, or just more people and customers, the watch stops or breaks. You've added more gears to the watch, but they don't all line up. They're out of sync. For us, simply beginning to offer a second product broke the watch. Our dependence on people no longer worked—we had to cross the line and embrace process because things became really complex really fast. It seems silly now that we didn't do it earlier."

Durand's analogy beautifully illustrates the risks and costs of an inattention to process. As things grow and change, relying exclusively on tribal knowledge (meaning, company information that lives only in employees' heads) becomes increasingly difficult. A leader's job is ensuring the gears in the watch are aligned, functioning properly, and telling time. Failure to do that well makes *everything* harder. The good news is the risks and costs caused by a lack of or inattention to process are completely avoidable and these benefits are more easily achieved than you might think. If you're ready, section II, *Learn*, will teach you exactly how to do that.

SECTION II

LEARN

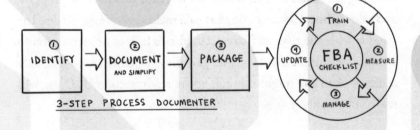

IDENTIFY → DOCUMENT AND SIMPLIFY → PACKAGE →

3-STEP PROCESS DOCUMENTER

① TRAIN
④ UPDATE — FBA CHECKLIST — ② MEASURE
③ MANAGE

CHAPTER 3

· · · · · · · · · · · · · · ·

OWN IT

The ability to learn is the most important
quality a leader can have.
—Padmasree Warrior, Founder & CEO, Fable

We hope that section I, *Commit* motivated you to face the problems, challenges, and lost opportunities caused by a lack of attention to and discipline for process. If so, you should now be ready to learn exactly how to document, simplify, and get your core processes followed by all. This section II, *Learn* provides a step-by-step guide and a complete set of simple concepts and practical tools being used by thousands of businesses around the world to do just that.

Using these tools and completing the steps outlined below takes the typical leadership team nine to twelve months. When you and your team have finished, you'll have a clear, simple blueprint for the exceptional results that your business or team can achieve on a consistent basis. To be successful, this journey must start with and be driven by you and your leadership team. Of course, you'll also collaborate with next-level managers and key individual contributors from time to time. However, you and your leadership team really need to own and drive this project.

That may surprise you, because many leaders think the best way to complete this work is to ask the person who's best at something to document that process. To be sure, involving others in this work is smart. Handing it off to them and bolting for the door is not.

Why?

Put yourself in the shoes of, say, your best salesperson. She's a rock star who does her own thing, hits her numbers every quarter, and is (generally) well-liked by customers and coworkers. She might be someone you personally trained, or perhaps she created the best practices on her own. Nonetheless, there are three reasons she's not the best person to document and simplify your sales process:

1. **She may not love the idea.** A top performer enjoys being a top performer. You're asking her to boil the important and unique work that she does every day down to a few essential steps. You explain that you plan to teach everyone else in the organization how to do it just as well as she does. If she's competitive at all (and find us a top sales performer who isn't), she may not fully commit to this project.

   One client tells the story of a top performer who agreed to help document a core process. He went home that night, flattered that the founder had asked him to help write down the important steps in what he does. When he recounted the conversation to his wife over dinner, her response surprised and frightened him, "He asked you to do *what*? You'd better take a cardboard box to work tomorrow. You're about to get fired!"

2. **She may struggle with the assignment.** To many top performers, consistent excellence comes naturally. Describing what they do and how they do it in a simple, straightforward way can be difficult. Many years ago, one of us asked a top salesperson how she won so much business at a trade show. "I don't know," she replied. "One minute I was at the bar getting to know some prospects. We weren't even talking about business. The next thing you know, every one of them wanted to buy something from us." While that's amusing, it's not exactly the kind of thing you can (or should) document, simplify, and get followed by all!

   Some top performers struggle in exactly the opposite way. They're too close to the ins and outs of their job to simplify things. They want to include every one-off step, exception to the rule, and "what about the time the prospect said that?" in the process. You're trying to document the way you *want* the sales process to go every time, not all of the possible variations—and that's often tough for an experienced team member.

3. **Her time will be better spent elsewhere.** It's likely your top performer loves what she does, is results driven, and wants to spend time acquiring new customers and growing relationships. Truth be told, it's in your company's best interests to keep her focused on that, too. By all means, leverage her expertise. Observe what she does and how she does it. Ask questions. Invite her to suggest ways to improve or streamline some of the steps—just don't pass the whole baton and expect her to run with it across the finish line.

You're almost certain to encounter resistance on your journey, so patience, determination, and real belief in the power of this work is critical every step of the way. Be willing to listen, learn, and lead in a way that builds your company's culture of discipline.

Every team needs a strong leader, and for this effort, that person needs to be passionate about process and skilled at keeping your team focused and accountable. For many organizations that describes the team's obvious leader—perhaps it's the business owner, CEO, president, or general manager. In a company running on EOS, it's often the Integrator, though on occasion it's a Visionary who's passionate about process.

If the team's obvious leader isn't the right driver of this project, find a leadership team member who does know and care about process. It may be the head of operations or finance, your finance leader, or even a process-oriented sales leader. You need someone knowledgeable and determined enough to overcome the challenges you'll face on the journey.

Now you have a skilled, energized team that owns it. You're all fully committed to the journey ahead. The path forward is simple and straightforward—though not always easy. It involves two EOS Tools (the **3-Step Process Documenter** and the **FBA Checklist**) as well as a bonus tool, **Getting What You Want**. These three tools and the tips we share to help you use them will be the focus of the next two chapters. Let's get started.

CHAPTER 4

• • • • • • • • • • • • • • •

THE 3-STEP PROCESS DOCUMENTER

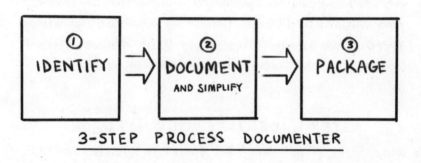

3-STEP PROCESS DOCUMENTER

What we're about to share with you may seem obvious or trivial. These are three very basic steps, but that doesn't mean they're ineffective. In fact, we believe their simplicity is what makes them work so consistently well in entrepreneurial companies. Many process improvement initiatives fail precisely because leaders fail to own, complete, or master the basics. They skip these simple steps altogether, or half-heartedly go through the motions rather than engaging fully in the work.

You cannot get the most important things in your business done consistently well if your leadership team is not 100 percent clear and on the same page. The 3-Step Process Documenter helps you agree on what those things are—your "handful of core processes." Then it helps you agree on the major steps within each process and explain the who/what/when/where/how of each step. Finally, it helps you figure out how best to package these core processes so they are easy to find and use.

When every leader in the company is aligned and eager to get these processes "followed by all," you'll change behavior more quickly and easily than you ever imagined was possible. Without that alignment and belief, you'll fail to overcome the mountain of resistance to even minor changes in "the way we've always done things" that exists in every organization. That's why this simple tool is so powerful.

STEP 1: IDENTIFY YOUR *HANDFUL* OF CORE PROCESSES

To some readers, this may seem like a five-minute exercise. Trust us: we've heard many a leadership team claim they "already know" what their core processes are. So, when we tell them the exercise actually takes about an hour, they are skeptical. Then we remind the team

that we need to identify and *agree* on a *handful* of core processes. Those two words—*handful* and *agree*—take the most time. When leadership teams do this exercise on their own (which happens most of the time), they come to understand. On the rare occasion that we're asked to facilitate for them, the exercise takes ... about an hour. Here's how it works:

We start by reminding everyone on the team that we're taking a 20/80 approach. Your people do a million different things every day, and we're not going to document and simplify all of it. We will focus our attention on a handful of core processes—five to twelve important things that you do repeatedly—which make your organization unique and valuable. What do you do that makes your organization a great place to work? What processes deliver terrific value to your customers? How do you hit deadlines, meet expectations, beat the competition, and make money? In other words, what are the ingredients in your business' *secret sauce*?

We then share with the team a sample list, saying, "A lot of companies have a list that includes an HR or people process, a marketing process, a sales process, and an account-management or customer-service process." Most companies have between two and five operations processes for how you build the product, deliver the service, manage your supply chain, and so on. Most companies also have an accounting process and a process for running the business (like EOS). When we're done, the whiteboard, flip chart, or online drawing tool looks like the following:

☐ HR
☐ MARKETING
☐ SALES
☐ ACCT. MGT./CUST. SVC.
☐ OPS 1
☐ OPS 2
☐ OPS 3
☐ ACCOUNTING
☐ RUNNING THE BIZ

This exercise is designed only to jump-start the team's thinking. It's not meant to be *your* list. We really just want each leader to think about what truly makes the organization consistently unique and valuable from their own perspective. With that context clear, ask each leader to take five quiet minutes to think and record their own list. "What would make *your* list of core processes?"

When we ask our team to spend "five quiet minutes," we sincerely mean "five" and "quiet." Letting the team think and work independently, without distraction, is important. People process differently, and many people need quiet time to gather their thoughts. This isn't the time to exchange ideas or process out loud yet. We'll collaborate shortly. Right now, we want to maximize the contribution of each team member and capture a broad range of perspectives.

After pens have stopped moving, compile the list on your whiteboard, flip chart, or drawing tool. Record the team's thoughts right next to the sample list you recorded earlier—where everyone can see it. It's extremely helpful for the team to see everyone's ideas laid out in a column, because you're about to walk them through a decision-making process, as follows:

1. Starting with the first item on the list, ask, "Is this one of our core processes?"

2. Facilitate the team to a decision—Yes or No
   - If Yes:
     ◦ Ask, "What should we call it (e.g., the HR process, the people process, etc.)?"
     ◦ Reach agreement. Make any change on the board.
   - If No:
     ◦ Ask, "Is this a major step in some *other* core process?"
     ◦ If No, cross out the item.
     ◦ If Yes:
       - Help the team decide which other process it belongs to or is a step in. For example, you may decide that "invoicing" is a step in the accounting process.
       - Cross out the item; draw an arrow to the relevant core process.
3. Go to the next item and repeat step 1.

When you finish the prioritization exercise, you'll end up with a list of core processes on the board that looks something like this:

HR PEOPLE
MARKETING
SALES
ESTIMATING
ORDER ENTRY
CUSTOMER SERVICE
ACCT. MGT
ENGINEERING
NEW PRODUCT DEV'T
PURCHASING
SUPPLY CHAIN MGT.
PRODUCTION   MANUFACTURING
LOGISTICS
INVOICING
ACCOUNTING
FACILITIES/EQUIPMENT
RUNNING THE BUSINESS
INVENTORY MGT

PRO TIPS: COMPLETING STEP 1

If you are the person leading step 1, here are some of our experiences to help you complete this exercise. It is unlikely that you'll get through this initial phase without getting stuck at least once—and that's okay. Here are the questions or concerns you may hear when people are struggling, along with the best strategies for resolving many of these obstacles:

- **"What's the difference between a core process and** _____**?"**

  We've gotten this question a thousand times, with dozens of words or phrases filling in that blank (e.g., procedure, SOP, non-core process, policy, major step, etc.). Remember that what you call these things matters less than the prioritization exercise you are facilitating. Don't get distracted spending time with your noses in a dictionary or thesaurus. Remind the team that you are just trying to identify the five to twelve *most important, repeatable processes* in the organization.

  If it isn't one of *those*, it isn't a core process. It may be a major step in a core process, or something else (and quite frankly, right now all that matters is that it's not a core process). Keep the team moving forward, focused on identifying your handful of core processes. Your mission is to *drive decisions* as you progress through each item on the compiled list. If necessary, ask for a little patience from team members who want the answer to every question right this minute.

- **"We have *way* more than five to twelve core processes."**

  At least one member of nearly every team is a genetically encoded lover of detail and complexity. A fellow EOS

Implementer shares the story of his client that manufactures, sells, and services *very* complicated machinery. The founder of the company balked when the Implementer told the team they could complete this first step in an hour.

"No way, wanna bet?" came the challenge. The Implementer agreed to the bet, promising to kiss the client's, um, tailgate if the exercise took more than sixty minutes.

"You better have your ChapStick handy," replied the confident founder. Sure enough, fifty-eight minutes later, the team completed this first step and the relieved Implementer won the bet.

When you're working through step 1 of the 3-Step Process Documenter, some people may list between fifteen and thirty-five core processes. Try to avoid getting frustrated by this level of detail or engaging in conflict right now. Patiently add every one of each person's items to the list on your whiteboard and trust that you'll pare down the complexity together.

The debate will occur naturally while you're trying to whittle the list down to your "handful." The high fact finders in the room may resist, noting for example, "We have fifteen different processes in accounting alone." The idea that one high-level accounting process with between five and twenty-five steps is enough for the 20/80 approach may bother them—a lot. Their list probably has an invoicing process, an A/R process, an A/P process, a financial-reporting process, a cash-management process, and so on.

That's actually a helpful debate, as long as everyone remembers that we're trying to keep things high level, simple, and crystal clear. Use detail to help align the team and make the right decision for *your company*. Ask, "Which approach do you think will create the simplest and clearest high-level guidelines for our employees? Having one accounting process that includes these other items as 'major steps'? Or having five distinct processes that go into far more detail?"

If you're facilitating this exercise and want to help the natural "complexifiers" on your team embrace the 20/80 approach, you can remind them that this work is just an executive summary. There's no rule preventing a leader who believes in a more detailed approach from building that over time. Here, just ask that the leader *start* with the high-level, 20/80 approach. After you agree on the major steps in the handful of core processes, your finance seat owner can build a more detailed, thorough set of procedures, policies, or SOPs.

- **Ready, Aim, Aim, Aim, Aim . . .**
Sir Winston Churchill said, "Perfection is the enemy of progress," and that is especially true in an entrepreneurial company. Lots of leaders suffer from perfectionism; it's both a blessing and a curse. On the one hand, that desire to be great is essential when you're growing a business or leading a high-powered team. When you're strengthening your Process Component, however, it can bring your efforts to a screeching halt.

Remind teams that you're doing the best job you can today with the information you have at hand. It doesn't need to be perfect or include every single step optimized for excellence. If you're afraid to launch anything until you have reached consensus on each step of every process, you will *never* launch. If you're battling that mentality during the step 1 exercise, simply remind participants that they may not nail it today, but they'll have ample opportunities to evolve and improve over time.

If your team is struggling with perfectionism, consider using an analogy to get them unstuck. Compare the organization to someone on a personal wellness journey. They want to get back in shape. They can research every eating plan from the grapefruit diet to vegan to paleo. They can interview the best trainers, coaches, and nutritionists. They can tour the best facilities and evaluate the latest in workouts, equipment, and even specific exercises. After all of that preparation, they'll know precisely *why* they're out of shape, and they may well have crafted a world-class plan to get back in shape. But they won't launch for months (or longer) . . . and we may well be speaking from personal experience here!

Another approach is to start with a single step in the right direction. Perhaps step on a scale regularly, with the goal of losing two kilograms each month or a pound every week. Maybe commit to a half-hour of exercise five days a week. Focus on getting a few major steps done consistently well and build from there. Pretty quickly, you will have optimized your wellness process until it's consistently delivering the results you want. Progress, not perfection.

You can make the same point by comparing the task at hand to teaching someone to play a musical instrument or teaching a child to play a sport. You start with the basics, patiently help them master those, and build from there. That's what we're doing here. Fight hard to help your team understand the power of simplicity and the value of mastering the basics. In the end, they'll determine what level of detail works best for them. The closer you can get to ready, aim, fire . . . the better.

- **What's the difference between a core process and a Proven Process?**
Leaders of companies running on EOS sometimes confuse two similar EOS terms. As you now know, a core process is something really important people within your organization should do repetitively to get a desired result. A Proven Process is part of your organization's marketing strategy. It's a one-page visual illustration of your ideal customer's experience from *their perspective*. Here's an illustration of EOS's Proven Process followed by companies implementing on EOS:

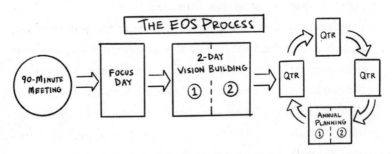

Strategic Coach founder Dan Sullivan refers to the difference between these two tools and perspectives as "front stage, back stage." Core Processes are designed to clarify and simplify the way you and your people work back stage, behind the scenes. A Proven Process is front stage. It's designed to illustrate the journey you want every customer to experience when they interact with you. Ultimately, following all of your backstage core processes will help deliver a consistent front stage Proven Process to your customers.

It matters what you call a thing.
—Solmaz Sharif, *Look: Poems*

One additional and important detail: Once you have decided what's truly a core process (and what isn't), get the team to agree on what you're going to call each of them, forever. This may seem trivial, but you need to present a united front to the rest of your organization. When leaders can't even agree what to call something important like a core process, it sends a message to everyone else that you're not at all on the same page. So, make a decision and agree on a name. Is it an "HR process," or a "people process?" Is it "sales" or "business development?" "Marketing" or "branding," or "lead generation?" Aligning around these "little things" creates clarity, efficiency, and alignment. Debate, agree, and be consistent.

Whatever decisions the team makes along the way is exactly right for your organization—even if you have a few more than twelve on your list. To complete step one of the 3-Step Process Documenter, simply ask a member of your team to turn the list from your whiteboard into a table of contents for the manual, drive, or video library that—someday soon—will house your handful of documented, simplified core processes. And move on to step two.

STEP 2: DOCUMENT AND SIMPLIFY
EACH CORE PROCESS

Simple can be harder than complex. You have to work
hard to get your thinking clean to make it simple.
—Steve Jobs

With your high-level list in hand—now
called your table of contents—you and
your team can begin the important
work of documenting and simplifying
your core processes. With your process
champion leading the discussion, start by
taking five to ten minutes to agree on a
high-level plan to document and simplify each core process. Ask
questions such as the following:

- Which process(es) should we document first?
- Who's going to document and simplify each core process?
- What should the final product look like?
- When will each process, as well as the entire project, be
  completed?

Let's unpack these questions one at a time. When prioritizing,
there are many factors to consider. Most teams first select the processes where they see the biggest potential for near-term return on
investment. If production errors, delays, and waste are out of control,
they start with the production or manufacturing process. If they're
struggling to attract or retain great people, they start with the HR,
people, or talent process. Occasionally a team decides to start with

one or more "easy" processes, what they might call "low-hanging fruit." There's nothing wrong with this approach, though you should know what *seems* easy does not always turn out that way.

Flow-Rite provides fluid-control systems and products for the marine, battery, hydroponic, and industrial markets. When the leadership team began documenting and simplifying their processes, the task seemed daunting at first. Shea Hickman, Flow-Rite's VP of human resources, wanted to preserve the team's enthusiasm for this work and score some early wins. "We prioritized the processes that involved everyone *or* would have the biggest near-term impact," she said. "We selected order intake because it affected all areas of the organization. Then we selected recruitment as well as our finance process to make the biggest impact first. This approach worked for us."

With priorities clear, identify one member of your team to lead the charge for each core process—sometimes called the *process owner*. This might be obvious—if you have a CFO or controller on the leadership team, that person will likely lead the effort to document and simplify the accounting process. Sometimes the choice is less clear. A customer-service process, for example, may involve people from every department in your organization. In that case, discuss each candidate and pick the leader most likely to coordinate the efforts of a cross-functional team and push the project over the finish line.

In either case, remember that the person leading the effort isn't doing all the work. They're simply accepting ultimate accountability for completing the project. They identify and gain commitment from the leaders and team members who can help make the project successful. They observe and listen well, coordinate the actions of all team members, and keep the project moving forward. If the project veers off track, they call the meetings, take the names, and, if necessary, kick the tails to get it back on track. Once a project team has created a draft of a documented and simplified core process, the project leader or process owner presents it to the leadership team for review, revision, and approval.

That begs the next question: "What should the final product look like?" Will it be a document, a workflow diagram, a series of images, or a video? It's difficult for the project leader to plan if he or she isn't clear on what "done" looks like. For help answering this question, consider the options referenced in *Step 3: Package* (on page 86).

Finally, make sure to set a timeline for documenting, simplifying, and getting each core process approved by the leadership team. For most teams, ninety days is the perfect timeline. Remember, it's a high-level, 20/80 approach. Ninety days allows ample time to assemble a team, observe and evaluate how things are being done today, look for ways to simplify or streamline the process, get feedback from the leadership team and/or key individual contributors on your first draft, and produce a final product.

EOS TIP: CORE PROCESSES, GOALS, AND ROCKS

A company running on EOS has a clear vision and plan, and it also excels at what we call "long-term predicting," or setting and achieving objectives. The EOS Tools that support setting and completing long-term objectives are a 1-Year Plan and Quarterly Rocks, which are a set of business priorities for the next 90 days.

The term Rocks is based on Stephen Covey's prioritization illustration in which students fill a glass cylinder (representing time) with water, sand, pebbles, and "big rocks." His lesson? That we leaders often struggle to get the truly important stuff (the Rocks) done (or into the cylinder) because we're overwhelmed by the urgent (everything else). So, setting and completing Rocks is all about prioritizing the truly important things first, and letting the other priorities (water, sand, pebbles) settle into the space between those priorities.

When a leadership team comes together every 90 days to review the prior quarter, get clear and aligned on the company's vision, and set new objectives for the coming quarter, they create a 90-Day World. Ultimately, this discipline is adopted by every team in the organization. Everyone is clear on the company's objectives and sets their own goals and Rocks to help the organization hit important measurables and follow-through on important priorities.

When a company running on EOS wants to strengthen its Process Component, that broader initiative often shows up as one of the three to seven goals in its 1-Year Plan. We insist on three to seven because less is more. When everything is important, nothing is important. Written SMART (specific, measurable, attainable, realistic, and timely), that goal might read, "Core processes documented, simplified, and FBA (followed by all)."

With priorities for the year set, leadership team members are reminded every 90 days to prioritize the Rocks that will help the team achieve the company's goals for the year. They first select Company Rocks (the three to seven most important priorities for *the company*), and then Individual Rocks (the three to seven most important priorities for *each leader*), including any Company Rock the leader owns).

So each quarter, documenting, simplifying, and getting a core process approved by the leadership team or completing one or more steps from the FBA Checklist might be a Company Rock or an Individual Rock. As noted above, when using this approach and these tools, our clients typically complete this project over nine to twelve months.

Whether you run your business on EOS or not, these principles will make you better at hitting your important measurables and completing your priorities. They will also help you strengthen your Process Component with discipline and accountability. Whether you call them Rocks or not, establish a clear owner, specific objective, and a reasonable timeline for each part of the larger project. Hold yourselves accountable for keeping things on track and for completing quality work on time. You'll be glad you did.

To acquire knowledge, one must study;
but to acquire wisdom, one must observe.
—Marilyn vos Savant

Once your plan is set, it's time to get started. If that seems daunting, begin the journey with a single step. Simply observe. This may seem indulgent or wasteful, but the best way to start documenting and simplifying a core process is by taking time to truly understand it, from start to finish. You can do this by "merely" observing.

You may have seen or heard of experienced process experts who figure everything out almost immediately when they walk into a factory, warehouse, or office. A disorganized pile of materials or a group of people standing around signals there's a bottleneck, delay, or inefficient workflow that needs to be fixed. We're not asking you to do that right now. Resist the temptation to change something—just be still and observe.

If you try to fix or optimize everything the first time you observe it, you'll never see the big picture—and you'll never finish. So, let go of any preconceived beliefs about how and why things are breaking today, or how things should be improved in the future. Just observe, remain curious, and note what you see.

The first thing you'll notice is whether a consistent way of doing it already exists. If there are eight people in sales doing it eight different ways, there is no process. That's a worthwhile observation that changes the nature of your mission. Building a model from scratch is different from fixing a broken process or improving an inefficient process. If there is an existing process, take the time to look through it, understand it, and compare it to what you observe when people are doing the work every day.

As you observe and learn, keep asking questions: What seems to be working? What's not? Does that happen every time or just occasionally? The way you ask these questions is important—be inquisitive rather than judgmental. "Why in the name of all that is holy are you doing it *that* way?" is an attack, not a question. Why questions, in general, tend to make people defend the *status quo*, whether they are attached to it or not.

Remember: this is scientific study. Feel free to take notes, make drawings, take pictures, or record a video. Observe and ask questions until you understand exactly what is being done, who's doing it, what's working, and what's not. When your observation is complete, you should have a good sense of what steps and methods seem to lead to the most positive outcomes. You'll have a list of issues too—points in the process when people are waiting around, bumping into one another, or making mistakes.

Once you've gained a solid understanding of the way things work today, evaluate what you learned. Look at what you've seen with a critical eye and a willingness to challenge "the way we've always done things."

If you're not sure how or where to start, watch the movie *The Founder*. It tells the origin story of McDonald's and is an excellent illustration of how to observe, evaluate, and ultimately improve a process until you have a well-oiled machine consistently producing the results you want. The movie has a great scene where Mac and Dick McDonald reflect on how they developed their processes to serve customers. It captures the brothers on a tennis court with clipboards, stopwatches, and diagrams galore—observing, evaluating, and experimenting. Their efforts resulted in the "Speedy System," a unique set of processes that helped McDonald's become the world's largest fast-food chain.

Let's break it down for those of you who don't own a restaurant or have a tennis court at your disposal. Simply gather your notes and ask yourself and key team members questions like these:

1. **What is the specific objective of this process?** Is the purpose of our marketing and sales processes to generate revenue from anyone willing to buy something from us? Or is it creating relationships with a business partner we'll be working with for years? For this effort to succeed, your answer must be crystal clear and shared by everyone on your leadership team.

2. **What's the first step in the process (and the last)?** Get clear yourself, and make sure your leadership team agrees. You may think the answer is obvious, but leaders have been arguing about where sales ends and account management or customer service begins for more than a hundred years.

3. **Are we consistently getting the results we want now?** If yes, just document best practices and look for little ways to simplify or streamline what's already working pretty well. If no, dig more deeply to identify the basic steps that, if repeated consistently, are most likely to produce exceptional results.

4. **What are the keys to success?** When you win a new target market customer or ship an order on time and to specifications, how did that happen? One of our clients noticed that the win rate on competitive bids was 34 percent when they met with clients in person before preparing those bids. It was only 19 percent when they did not. That discovery turned into an

essential major step in their sales process, and an important measurable on their sales team's Scorecard.

5. **What causes problems?** Where did you observe delays, bottlenecks, mistakes, missed handoffs, duplicated effort, and so on? This is where you'll simplify the process by eliminating, streamlining, or automating steps. One of our clients, a designer and manufacturer of plastic parts, noticed a step in one of their processes that required four people to grab and place a large sheet of plastic on a molding machine. That observation/evaluation led them to purchase a robot that fully automated the step. Reductions in labor expense and costly errors caused by this manual process covered the cost of the machine in less than fifteen months.

If you can't explain it simply, you don't understand it well enough.
—Albert Einstein

Based on what you've learned through observation and evaluation, it's now time to document and simplify the process. Keep this work at a high level. You're focused on the major steps, the 20 percent that delivers 80 percent of the results. A major step is one of the five to twenty-five things you need to get right every time to get great results. Putting together an attractive compensation and benefits package is probably a major step in your people process. Figuring out which font to use in your employee handbook is not.

For each major step, briefly explain the who, what, when, where, and how with a series of substeps, which some people refer to as procedures or standard operating procedures (SOPs). If you're using a step-by-step checklist (one of many ways to document and simplify a process), the major step will be followed by two to five bullets. They provide clarity, but at a much higher level than the detailed SOP manuals that many organizations compile and then rarely use.

The goal is a simple and clear explanation of the major steps in a process that will immediately help a new employee consistently execute the basics of his or her job. Think one-page checklist, not three-ring binder. If you can't describe a process clearly and simply enough to achieve that result, either your process is too complex, or you need to understand and explain it better. See the sample on the next page of a documented and simplified HR process.

In *The Checklist Manifesto: How to Get Things Right*, surgeon and best-selling author Atul Gawande illustrates the impact that a simple checklist can make on even the most complex of processes. He cites examples from high-stakes operations like hospitals, airlines, and construction companies. Even for seasoned experts with thousands of hours of training and experience like doctors, nurses, and airline pilots, Gawande proves that using simple checklists covering the absolute basics will vastly reduce critical and sometimes fatal mistakes.

Johns Hopkins Hospital, for example, instituted a five-step checklist to reduce the infection rate among ICU patients when using central-line catheters:

1. Wash your hands.
2. Clean the patient's skin.
3. Wear protective coverings and put sterile drapes over the patient.
4. Avoid placing a catheter in the groin where infection rates are higher.

THE H/R PROCESS

The Search
- Define role/job description/salary (the seat in the Accountability Chart™)
- Decide search medium
- Begin search
- E-mail blast to sphere/peers

Interviewing
- Screen résumés
- Initial interview/profiling tools
- 2nd interview
- Check references
- CEO interview

Hiring
- 8-hour on-the-job trial
- Decision
- 90-day trial

Orientation
- H/R policy/review employee manual
- Benefits review/forms
- Job training
- CEO orientation (company story/core ideology)

Quarterly Conversations
- What's working, what's not?
- Review the 5-5-5™/People Analyzer™ (RPRS)
- Review LMA questionnaires
- Delegate and elevate opportunities
- Update Accountability Chart if necessary

Annual Reviews
- Manager fills out People Analyzer, including GWC™ in preparation for the review
- Document the review and have it signed by all parties
- File the review with the H/R department

Termination
- 3-strike system (30-30-30)
- Terminate upon 3rd strike
- Contact legal counsel
- Meet with employee/have H/R present
- Exit interview
- Document termination and have it signed by all parties

5. Remove the catheter as soon as possible, even if there's a chance it might be needed again at some point.

Before the checklist project, the median rate of central-line infections in Michigan was about three per one thousand catheter-hours, above the national average. After eighteen months, most Michigan ICUs reported *none* of these bloodstream infections.

"Prior to our work, we thought these were largely inevitable infections and that they were simply a cost of being in the hospital," says the study's sponsor, Peter Pronovost, a professor of anesthesiology and critical care medicine at the university's School of Medicine. "Now we know they are universally preventable. We've reset the benchmark."

Similarly, the World Health Organization (WHO) introduced a safe surgery checklist in eight different cities around the world. Notably, this checklist focused exclusively on basic, repeatable steps, not the areas where independent judgment was required, such as during surgery.

SURGICAL SAFETY CHECKLIST

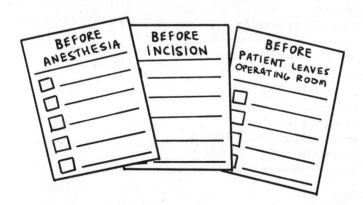

Implementing the new process reduced the rate of major complications in all eight hospitals by 36 percent. Gawande shares, "Deaths fell 47% . . . infections fell by almost half. Overall, in this group of nearly four thousand patients, 435 would have been expected to develop serious complications. Using the checklist spared more than 150 people from harm—and 27 of them from death."

In aviation, preflight checklists were first introduced in the 1930s. They have had a profound impact on reducing both in-flight failures and pilot errors ever since. According to NTSB data, each year the failure to use checklists is a frequent factor in airplane crashes. Moreover, best practices mandate that a checklist include the minimum items to ensure safety, and be written in clear, concise language. The philosophy behind this approach? The more user-friendly a process is, the more it will be used.

Even if mistakes aren't fatal in your business, simple and useful tools like checklists can make a big difference in the way you serve team members and customers. So, resist the temptation to "complexify." Align your leadership team around the basics first. Help your people master those basics until doing the important stuff the right way becomes routine, almost automatic. Then build from there.

Be prepared for pushback. Some leaders and individual contributors will fight your attempts to document and simplify what they do every day. Some are detail-oriented perfectionists. They don't understand how anything simple and high level could possibly make a difference. For others, it's a matter of personal pride. They've spent years "mastering their craft" and the suggestion that everything they've learned can be summarized in a handful of repeated steps is hard to swallow.

Stay the course. Ask the leaders pleading for more detailed SOPs, procedures, or policies for a little trust and patience. Let them know these high-level checklists are just a great place to start. Tell them that this approach has worked beautifully for thousands of companies and tens of thousands of leaders. Assure them that if getting them followed by all doesn't consistently produce the desired results, you'll consider a more detailed approach.

Assure those whose egos may be bruised by this approach that you respect and value their expertise. Agree with (or at least tolerate) their assertion that every sales opportunity, or new product development project, or even every financial report—is unique and different. Let them know that you're merely trying to document the major steps that we should work hard to follow every single time. Explain that you're counting on their God-given talent, years of experience, and considerable skill to fill in the blanks or adjust when there's a legitimate reason that we can't or shouldn't follow the process.

PRO TIPS: COMPLETING STEP 2

1. **Use an EOS Tool Called** *Getting What You Want.* We've
    seen leaders and teams use all sorts of methods to document
    their core processes—from scribbling notes on a legal pad to a
    formal business-process management (BPM) session involving
    a team, lots of Post-it notes, and a long, smooth wall on which
    to hang your work. Whatever your team thinks will work best
    for them is fine, but the simpler the better. If you want to
    take a deeper dive into Business Process Model and Notation
    (BPMN) visit the Object Management Group's website (with
    one of the best acronyms we've seen yet) at *omg.org.*

    When a leader or team struggles with step two, we suggest
    an EOS Tool called *Getting What You Want*—a simplified
    version of a more complex BPM session. See the complete tool
    on page 153.

Example 1	Add Target Prospect to List	Make Contacts	First Meeting	Needs Assessment	Create Proposal	Present Proposal	What Do You Want? 1 New Client/MO
	8 / WK	4 / WK	2 / WK	1 / WK	2 / MO	2 / MO	

If you look closely at this tool, along with the example provided, you'll see it directs you to begin at the end by asking "What Do You Want?" at the end of a process. Work together throwing out ideas, narrowing down your list, and clarifying things until that outcome is stated clearly, simply, and specifically. Ensure you all agree. Until that happens, trying to document and simplify a core process is like herding cats.

Included with the tool is an example—a sales process. The desired result of that process is to win one new client. From there, we work backward, only recording the steps we agree *must* be done well in order to produce the desired outcome. Let's illustrate that with something other than what's captured in the tool itself. And just to lighten things up, let's use an example from everyday life. Let's make some toast.

- Last step—plate two buttered pieces of toast
- Prior step—apply butter to warm toast
- Prior step—remove from toaster
- Prior step—toast ejected from toaster
- Prior step—depress toaster lever
- Prior step—place two pieces of fresh bread in toaster

Hearty thanks to Tom Wujec for the inspiration. His "draw toast" design exercise, described in detail at *drawtoast.com*, helps teams get better at understanding and solving complex problems. It's a collaborative, effective, and *fun* way to help your team design and agree on a core process that will produce a consistently exceptional result. One of the teams he worked with illustrated the list of steps above that resulted in a diagram similar to the one following:

Bringing it back to a business example, let's use the *Getting What You Want* tool to document and simplify the hiring step in our people process. Yes, you *can* use this EOS Tool to think through one or more major steps in any of your core processes.

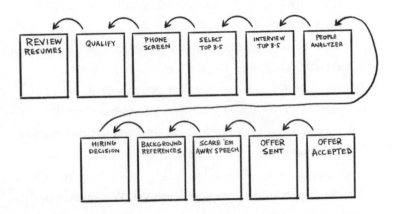

Beginning at the end is a helpful technique for minimizing complexity. We're not trying to identify *every* step that *might* happen during the step or process, we're documenting the *necessary* steps. Yes, some candidates may not accept our initial offer, requiring us to repeat a few steps or improvise. But if we try to build all those one-offs, ad hocs, and what-ifs into every process or major step, then we'll be *drowning* in complexity and never get clarity on the right high-level process.

The *Getting What You Want* tool is also quite helpful when working through the "*Measure*" item on the FBA Checklist (see chapter 5, page 99). Specifically, it can help you identify leading indicators—activities-based numbers that predict future results. That makes it easier to decide which steps to measure, and what the goal might be for each measurable. With the sales process illustration on the tool above, for example, a salesperson who wants to close one new deal per month might hold himself accountable for identifying eight prospects per week, contacting four, meeting with two, conducting one needs assessment per week, and sending a proposal every two weeks.

These leading indicators help the salesperson and his manager react more quickly to keep things on track. He can react in week one if any of those numbers are off track rather than waiting until the end of the month and realizing he hasn't closed a deal. That's the power of process. It can drive accountability for hitting leading, activities-based numbers, and the *Getting What You Want* tool can help you decide what to measure and where to set the goals.

2. **Leadership Team Review and Approval.** Whatever approach, tool, or format you choose, draft a documented, simplified core process to share with your leadership team. Next, meet with them to thoroughly review and approve the draft. This is an essential step for three reasons:

- **To get the process right.** Your leadership team is the most experienced and knowledgeable group of people in the business. When you walk through a process step-by-step, and give them a chance to ask questions, poke holes, and suggest improvements, the end product will be far better. Ken Blanchard, author of the *One Minute Manager*, reminds us, "None of us is as smart as all of us."

- **To be 100 percent on the same page.** To drive change and accountability, you'll need to rely on the support of your fellow leaders. When they understand the process and think it's the right way to do things, they'll join you in driving accountability for following it. They'll also be more likely to trust that you're leading and managing your people well, and fully capable of solving issues as they arise. This alignment leads to less second-guessing, fewer end runs, and a more unified, healthy leadership team.

- **To save time.** When mistakes occur, many leadership teams waste countless hours debating *why* it occurred. A company struggling to hire great people, for example, might spend days, weeks, or years trying to decide whether to blame the tight labor market, the way the job posting was written, where it was posted, internal or external recruiters, the hiring manager—you name it!

  This almost always boils down to a debate: Is it your people or your process? When the team is certain a process is documented, simplified, and being followed by all, that circular argument simply *does not happen.* The fact that you recently reviewed and approved the process, trained your people, and started measuring and managing both actions and results instills confidence. Now you can look at the data and see where the process is breaking down, what's causing those breakdowns, and fix it. You can solve the issue at the root, for the long-term and greater good of the organization.

So, before you finalize and roll out a core process, ask your colleagues to thoroughly review and approve it. With the 20/80 approach, you're shooting for a one- to five-page document or clear simple workflow, series of images, or video. Please don't ask your team to review and approve a seventy-five-page procedural manual. Most of our teams find the following approval process works well:

- Share the documented, simplified process with each member of your team one week before a meeting at which you plan to review, revise (if necessary), and approve the process.
- Ask everyone to come prepared with questions, comments, or issues.
- Walk through the process one step at a time, reviewing each substep or bullet.
- Answer questions and resolve issues as you go.
- Conclude the meeting with a marked-up copy of the process and a deadline for producing a final copy.

Once your leadership team has reviewed and approved each of your company's core processes, you're ready for step three of the 3-Step Process Documenter: Package.

STEP 3: PACKAGE (MAKE THEM EASY TO FIND AND USE)

Real change, enduring change, happens one step at a time.
—Ruth Bader Ginsburg

Now that you've documented, simplified, and approved your core processes, the next step is rolling them out to the entire organization. Most teams do this when the whole process manual is complete. Some roll them out one at a time, or in small batches. Before presenting them to the people doing the work every day, focus on ease of use. Specifically, how can you package the final product so employees can easily find them, use them, and incorporate them into their daily routines?

FIND THE RIGHT FORMAT, MEDIUM, OR PLATFORM

Start by thinking about the kind of work your people do every day. What format or medium best fits that kind of work? Also consider when, where, and how your people will be using these tools. Are they in the office or out in the field? Are they looking at a screen all day or in the field working with their hands under varying conditions? Will a document serve them best? A checklist on a smartphone or tablet? A video they can watch repeatedly? Pick the tool and platform most likely to be simple, practical, and useful to the people who will be following the core process every day.

We've seen processes packaged as simple, bulleted documents that are printed or stored in a well-structured online directory. We've seen workflows, sequential images, and screenshots with notes, as shown in the examples below. Note that each example is constructed in a way that makes the final tool easy for any employee who interacts with the process to understand and use.

Many organizations have turned to video content, stored on generic platforms such as YouTube or Vimeo or on video-library platforms specifically built for processes, like PlaybookBuilder, Trainual, or Whale. These tools and others like them leverage the latest in learning science, like reinforcement and gamification, to engage employees in the journey to master core processes.

As technology advances, options will become more varied and advanced. A recent collaboration between Ford Motor Company and the Bosch Group used virtual reality headsets to train technicians on the all-electric Ford Mustang Mach-E, the company's first all-electric SUV. Without access to physical vehicles, technicians at Ford dealerships around the world were trained to replace batteries and complete repairs on vehicles and parts they'd never seen before, so when the Mach-E came to their shops they would know what to do. This unique approach to training saved time and money while increasing quality and customer satisfaction. It also upgraded the capabilities of service technicians around the globe in a fun and interesting way.

MAKE THEM EASY TO FIND

Now that you've selected the right format, platform, or medium, let's make these valuable tools so easy to find and use that they're always available. How can we locate them as close to where the work is being done as possible? How can we organize each process so that employees can quickly and reliably access exactly what they're looking for? According to a study published in Marie Kondo's *Joy at*

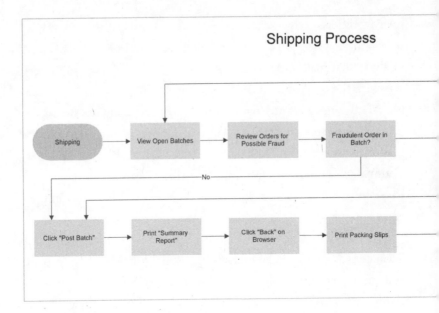

Shipping Process

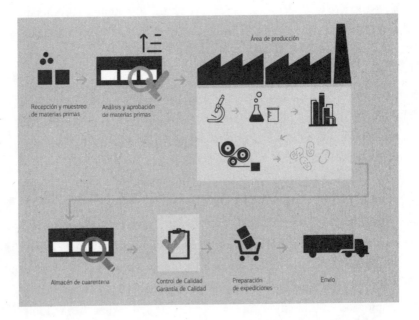

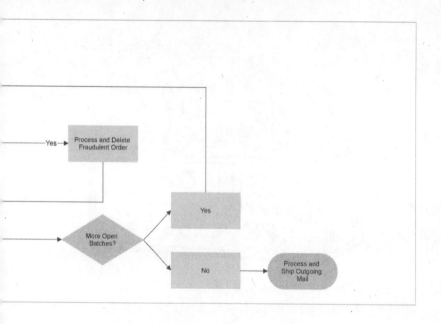

Work, employees spend 20 percent of their time each week just looking for information—that's one full workday each week!

This fact was confirmed in a recent session with a successful, rapidly growing property management firm. One of their quarterly Rocks was "Core processes documented, simplified, and approved by the leadership team." When reviewing the completion status of the prior quarter's Rocks, the team's operations leader and process champion quickly and proudly said, "Done!" Half the team looked confused.

"How can that be done?" asked the founder.

"I sent everybody an email with a link to our intranet site," said the operations leader.

Ten minutes later, after a thorough search through the site, the whole team saw a complete set of well-documented and beautifully illustrated core processes. Relieved, the operations leader took a Rock the following quarter to make the processes *much* easier to find.

How you and your team decide to do that depends on how each process is packaged and how and where the work is being done. If you've settled on a printed set of core processes, include a date of last update on each process and make plenty of copies. Place them throughout the facility, as close to the work as possible. If your processes are being used in a production shop or distribution center, consider large format graphics, hung from the ceilings or mounted on the wall. Ensure they're clearly visible for the employees who are doing that process. If your processes are being accessed via desktop, laptop, tablet or smartphone, use an intuitive, searchable platform and a commonsense organizational structure.

We've seen companies do this well on basic platforms such as their existing file management systems, including an intranet site, Sharepoint, OneDrive, or GoogleDocs. We've seen teams use more specialized tools like Asana, Trello, Whale, Trainual, Notion, or PlaybookBuilder. Whatever format or platform you choose, remember that it's not the tool you've got—it's what you do with it. If your people can't find it, they won't use it.

It's also important to make a process easy to see, read, and *use*. On documents, favor crystal clear words or short phrases rather than long, complex sentences. On checklists and workflow documents, use color, common symbols, and large print so employees can follow the visuals with a quick glance. On a production floor or distribution center, use lighting, color coding, and images that make your processes visible and useful from where the work is being performed.

Visual Factory is a lean concept that places valuable information throughout the workplace. It's a simple, effective system of communication tools used to share information at the time and place it is needed. The approach relies on color, lighting systems, workflow diagrams or process illustrations, clearly labeled workstations and bins, and data or status updates displayed in real time. It keeps team members informed and work flowing smoothly through a process. Here's a lighthearted example:

You don't have to run a factory or distribution center or even operate as a lean organization to benefit from applying these principles. For example, a successful roofing contractor uses clearly marked, color-coded bins to keep their sales and delivery processes moving forward. They are affixed to a wall visible to every team member.

The person who takes a call from a prospective customer follows a basic process to capture the information necessary to understand and describe the opportunity. When complete, a clearly defined opportunity ticket is placed in the first bin. An estimator retrieves the ticket, schedules and completes the inspection, and produces an estimate. When the estimate is approved, the ticket moves to the scheduling bin, and so on—all the way through to project completion. Every team member knows the workflow and can see the bins as they're filled and emptied throughout the day. Each feels accountable to empty the bin for the steps they own in the process. As a result, the company's pace, conversion rates, and customer satisfaction have all increased dramatically.

Whatever format and platform you choose, make the finished product a simple, complete blueprint for effective day-to-day execution in your business. That's the purpose of a process manual, even if it's not in an actual manual. As noted earlier, it's what Gerber referred to as your "Franchise Prototype" in *The E-Myth Revisited*. The final step in this process is giving your blueprint or operating model a name—something accurate, memorable, and maybe even compelling. Many of our clients refer to their set of core processes as "[Our Company] Way" or "[Our Company] Playbook." Feel free to get creative. One client named the manual "XYZ Company's Secret Sauce," another the "Circle of Life," and yet another the "ABC Company DNA."

You've now completed the 3-Step Process Documenter. Your core processes are documented, simplified, approved by your leadership team, and packaged in a way that makes them easy for your people to find and use. Now it's time to use another EOS Tool that will help you get your handful of core processes "followed by all" or "FBA."

- - - - - - - - - - - -

CHAPTER 5

THE FBA CHECKLIST

> Even if you are on the right track, you'll
> get run over if you just sit there.
> **—Will Rogers**

You and your team have just completed a ton of really important work, but the journey is far from over. This next step—getting those core processes followed by all—is both challenging and vital. Often process work comes to an uneremonious end at this stage, with first-rate process manuals becoming obsolete almost overnight. It's a shame and completely unnecessary.

Erik Piasio of American Surgical Company noted this important difference. "We are in a highly regulated industry, so we had a lot of processes documented," he shared. "Using EOS's FBA Checklist, however, helped us make sure that the processes were actually being used by everyone, which changed the entire culture of our company."

To begin consistently getting the results you want, you must permanently change the way people do things in your business. Completing a four-step checklist and then repeating that checklist regularly is all that's required. First, *Train* every employee who performs one or more steps in a core process. Next, *Measure* performance to ensure people are doing things right, doing them often enough, and getting the desired result. Third, *Manage* in a way that drives real accountability, and finally, *Update* each process regularly to stay current and continue improving.

Let's take them one at a time:

- **Train** every employee who performs one or more steps in each process. When we say, "every employee," we mean *every* employee, from brand-new team members to your most-seasoned veterans. *Everyone* must have a chance to walk through the process, ask clarifying questions, and even push back or poke holes. When your team truly understands each step in the process as well as the big picture, they'll be more likely to help you move forward rather than digging their heels in.

  The methods for training are also diverse and ever-changing. Analyze your audience carefully and pick the approach that matches the needs of the team being trained.

You should also consider what would provide the best return on your investment of time and money. If you and your team have a regular Meeting Pulse (see box below), you may be able to complete the initial training without adding another meeting.

EOS TIP: THE MEETING PULSE

The leadership team of a company running on EOS gains traction—the ability to execute on the company's vision with discipline and accountability—with a two-part Meeting Pulse. The first part is the 90-Day World we referenced in the EOS Tip about setting and completing Rocks (see page 68). The second part is a weekly Level 10 Meeting that keeps the organization moving forward within the quarter—hitting its numbers, completing priorities, keeping customers and employees happy, and solving issues.

Once the leadership team masters this two-part Meeting Pulse, it's rolled out to the entire organization one level at a time. Ultimately, every team and employee lives in a 90-Day World and engages in its own Level 10 Meeting. Departmental Level 10 Meetings are typically shorter and more tactical, but they follow the same agenda. Having this time set aside weekly for important priorities (like training on a core process) is a great way to keep people aligned on your vision, clear on their priorities, and accountable for keeping things on track and consistently producing exceptional results.

You may have to schedule one or more formal training sessions. You may decide to train people one-on-one, by going on a "ride-along" or role-playing with each salesperson, for example. You might use your cellphone and collect videos of best practices (and maybe bloopers) in action. A growing number of companies use online training programs with robust learning management systems to track progress.

A husband and wife team run their publishing company, Local Profile, on EOS. They shared an amusing and impactful story about the benefits of using documented processes for training. From the start, Phillip Silvestri was a huge fan of getting processes documented in their business. Rebecca Silvestri, VP of Sales and Marketing—not so much. After a lot of give and take and "demand and avoid," Rebecca agreed to write the processes for the sales and marketing team that she was leading. As a compromise, she opted to use the 20/80 approach to document and simplify the process—instead of the complexity her detail-loving business partner sought.

After seamlessly training her team, Rebecca emailed her EOS Implementer to celebrate the impact of the tools she created: "We recently onboarded a new team member into sales, and because we have all the major steps in our sales process documented, she was fully effective in her role after two weeks and just three to four training sessions. Because we had a clearly defined process to teach from, each training session flowed naturally, ran smoothly, and was completed on time. Additional help since the training has been minimal since she's able to refer back to the documented process."

Whatever method you choose, make sure everyone's trained. Conclude the training event(s) by verifying that they understand each step in the process, as well as the description your process provides of the who/what/where/when and how. Gain their commitment for following the process, and offer continued training, help, and support. You need that commitment from your people, and they'll need your support and occasional redirection, because as we know, old habits die hard.

That's not just an idiom—it's a proven fact. *Training Industry Magazine* explains that training alone won't change behavior, largely due to something called the "forgetting curve." This theory was introduced in the late nineteenth century by German psychologist Hermann Ebbinghaus, who discovered and documented the human brain's difficulties retaining new information after even short periods of time. Subsequent studies suggest that we forget up to 90 percent of new information within thirty days, and 70 percent of that loss happens within the first twenty-four hours!

Two great ways to reinforce training, increase retention, and truly change behaviors are the next two steps in the FBA Checklist—measure and manage.

- **Measure** to reinforce training and change behaviors. Determine which steps in each process to measure and exactly what type of measurement makes sense for each step— compliance, frequency, or outcomes. In other words, are they doing it right, are they doing it often enough, or are they getting the desired result? Let's look at those three types of measurement one at a time:

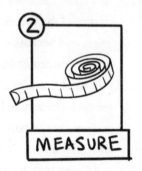

- Measuring *compliance* means verifying that the person performing a step in the process did it the right way. If the step requires an operator to put on safety goggles before turning on the CNC machine, for example, you would record and report any instances of non-compliance.

- Measuring *frequency* means checking to see if the step is repeated often enough to get the desired result. Take the case of the salesperson who needs to generate one new order per week to meet the company's expectations. If her closing ratio is 33 percent, that means she needs to present three proposals per week to generate the desired outcome of one new order.

- Measuring *outcomes* means verifying that you are getting the results that you want. Putting on safety goggles is one step in a process designed to improve safety and prevent accidents or incidents. Measuring those things is important too, because following a process isn't helpful in the least if it doesn't produce the results you want.

To be clear, we're not telling you to measure every major step in each core process using each of these three methods. There will be some steps you don't measure at all, and others that are critical to measure and monitor regularly. You will find some steps are easier to measure than others. You will find some steps more valuable to measure because they are better leading indicators—they do a better job predicting future results.

For each step you *do* decide to measure, pick the method that works best from the three options above. If doing it right is really important, consider measuring for compliance. If doing it frequently enough is critical, measure for frequency. Don't be afraid to take a shot—you'll dial in your approach to measuring for compliance, frequency, and outcomes over time.

There are many ways to gather these three kinds of data. The most obvious is personal observation. You can walk through the plant regularly and record a tick mark every time you see a machine operator not wearing goggles or hand out gift cards to those who *are* wearing goggles. This may sound silly or wasteful, especially if it requires the time and energy of high-paid members of the leadership team. But it really works.

> If you cannot measure it, you cannot improve it.
> **—Lord Kelvin**

Sometimes, things improve precisely *because* you're measuring it. The CEO for one client—a distribution company whose trucks completed several runs per day—got tired of hearing his operations manager say that reducing truck turnaround time from sixty-seven to thirty minutes was "impossible." The following Monday, the resolute CEO stood on the loading dock with a stopwatch and a clipboard. When someone asked him what he was doing, he simply said, "Measuring truck turnaround time." Not surprisingly, he noticed that the driver walked away with a little more pep in his step.

Another driver asked him what the goal was. "Thirty minutes," he replied, and again, he noticed the driver start moving a little faster. As word spread, the other drivers picked up the pace as well. They started asking for help from the material handlers and other warehouse and yard personnel.

By the end of the week, average turnaround time was down to forty minutes. At this point, the whole team became engaged, looking for ways to streamline and simplify various steps in the company's process. Within four months, the company had achieved its goal, saving nearly $100,000 per year in down time and increasing customer satisfaction to boot.

You can also ask people to self-count or self-report. Many world-class safety organizations have proven that people aligned with a goal are willing to admit mistakes and omissions for the greater good. A company running on EOS that produces a broad range of outdoor canvas products, significantly reduced errors in their shop by placing whiteboards near each workstation. Employees were encouraged to place a tick mark on the whiteboard when they made an error. This required a significant cultural shift that the leaders supported by celebrating those who self-reported consistently. They even gave spot rewards, handing cash or gift cards to employees they observed putting a tick mark on the whiteboard.

Another way to measure the success of a process is an EOS Tool that has helped thousands of companies: The Company Scorecard.

EOS TIP: THE (WEEKLY) SCORECARD

The leadership teams of companies running on EOS spend five minutes each week reviewing a Company Scorecard in their weekly Level 10 Meeting (described in the EOS

Tip on page 97). A great Scorecard contains 5–15 leading indicators that give teams an absolute pulse on the business and the ability to predict future results. As a result, leaders can react more quickly to off-track measurables rather than waiting for the results to come in at the end of a month or a quarter. (See a larger version of this tool on page 163.)

Who	Measurable	Goal	Weeks													
			1	2	3	4	5	6	7	8	9	10	11	12	13
Sue	New leads	36	11	4	47	17	29	24	35	41					
Sue	Initial sales meetings	12	8	9	4	14	11	15	16	13					
Sue	Proposals (#)	4	2	1	3	4	2	4	5	4					
Sue	Proposals ($)	$300K	$175K	$70K	$275K	$350K	$150K	$370K	$410K	$325K					
Sue	30-day pipeline	$1.5M	$1.15M	$1.05M	$1.10M	$1.25M	$1.15M	$1.05M	$1.10M	$1.25M					
Sue	Contracts (#)	2	2	1	1	2	3	1	3	4					
Sue	Contracts ($)	$150K	$161K	$135K	$75K	$170K	$201K	$41K	$170K	$320K					
Evan	Projects late	1			4	4	4	3	3	4					
Evan	Projects over budget	1							2	2					
Evan	Defects to clients	0		1		1	0	2	1	1					
Evan	Utilization rate	80%													
Carol	Cash balance	$75K	$55K	$85K	$70K	$61K	$52K	$91K	$77K	$68K					
Carol	A/R > 60 days	< $30K	$42.5	$42.5	$31.0	$26.1	$35.5	$40.5	$34.0	$36.4					
Carol	Billing errors	0	0	1	1	0	0	1	1	0					

As mentioned above, a *leading indicator* is an activities-based number that, when repeated properly, produces a desired result. Since a core process is, by definition, a series of steps that produce a desired result, the major steps in each process become great measurables on an effective Scorecard. This synergy is why so many of our clients discover that strengthening their company's Process Component *also* helps them strengthen their company's Data Component.

One client shared that before strengthening their Process Component, they questioned the value of expensive trade shows but often attended them nonetheless. The company's new sales process, and the measurements they implemented around major steps, helped clarify the issue. First, the process ensured the company prepared for, engaged in, and followed up on these shows properly. Their Scorecard set reasonable expectations for leads generated and sales made. After months of tracking the data, the team was able to see clearly that a big booth at the trade show was not worth the investment. Instead, the process and the data confirmed what several members of the leadership team had suspected all along. Attending trade shows and actively networking with customers and prospects made sense. Investing heavily in a booth and related expenses did not.

Technology and automation can make all three kinds of measurements more efficient, accurate, and useful. Software for enterprise resource planning (ERP), customer relationship management (CRM), and accounting systems top the list. It's not unusual for high-tech plants to be equipped with cameras and sensors that detect and weed out defective parts before they come off the line. Large produce growers often have a machine on their packing line that not only detects defects, it removes blemished fruit or vegetables before they can be packaged and sent to market.

Once you figure out what to measure and how to measure it, remember the 20/80 approach. Less is more. Pick a *handful* of numbers you think will tell a complete story about how you are performing relative to the expectations set by each process. Use the most efficient way to gather that data, and regularly review the results with your team. Whether you're running on EOS or not, regularly ensuring important numbers are "on track" and responding accordingly when they are off track is essential.

Which brings us to the next item in the FBA Checklist.

- **Manage**—or what a company running on EOS calls "LMA," which stands for leadership, management, and accountability. Training your people is important, measurement provides reinforcement, but effective leadership and management is truly the key to changing behaviors and ensuring each of your core processes is followed by all.

> Effective leadership is putting first things first. Effective management is discipline, carrying it out.
>
> **—Stephen Covey**

By prioritizing the important work of documenting and simplifying your core processes, you've led by introducing a new order of things in your organization. You began driving discipline with training and by reinforcing that training with measurement. Now it's time for everyone who leads and manages in your organization to turn this new way of doing things into automatic habits, thus creating what Jim Collins described as a *culture of discipline*.

Start by giving clear direction. Help your people understand why this new way of operating is valuable and how succeeding will benefit not only the company but also every one of its employees. When they resist or complain, listen carefully and seek to understand their concerns. As Dwight Eisenhower once said, "You don't lead by hitting people over the head. That's assault, not leadership." Reiterate the reasons for changing, encourage them to keep trying, and offer to support them along the way.

Provide team members with the necessary tools to permanently change their behavior. Can they easily access the process document, checklist, or video? Can they receive additional training if necessary? Do they know who to contact when they're confused or stuck? Have you made *yourself* available so that each of your direct reports has enough of your time and attention to integrate this change into their daily routine?

Make sure your expectations are reasonable and clear. You can't expect them to master this new way of doing things overnight. You're measuring compliance, frequency, and outcomes, maybe for the first time. That can be scary for employees not accustomed to using data to get better every day. They may feel you're doing it to catch them making mistakes, which can reduce their level of confidence or create resentment. That's why it's so important to set realistic goals and coach rather than punish when you don't see immediate results. In short, be clear, firm, kind, and patient. If you've changed the way someone does their job or the culture of your company and expect 100 percent compliance right away, that expectation is unrealistic and demotivating.

Your team members also have expectations of you and of the organization. In most modern work environments, successful leadership and management is a two-way street. It's important that you ask each individual what *they* need on this journey, and work hard to meet their reasonable expectations.

This feedback may involve a request for additional tools or changes to the work flow for greater efficiency. For example, an employee of one client asked their supervisor to buy additional trash cans so that he and his crew could discard scrap materials. He also asked that they place the new cans in a location that was closer to his team's work station. This small but important change had many benefits, including improved productivity and morale. When your team's questions, concerns, and constructive feedback are healthy and reasonable, work hard to meet those expectations.

As you may have guessed, communicating well is critical during this transition to a new way of doing things. Speak clearly and be comfortable repeating yourself often. Perhaps more importantly, listen well. Seek to understand and appreciate your team members as they progress through this transition. Don't fall prey to assumptions—validate understanding every step of the way rather than assuming your people have everything they need, or vice versa.

Lastly, make sure you're doing a great job of providing positive and constructive feedback to your team. When they do things right, do them often enough, and get the desired results—are you celebrating with them as visibly as possible? When they make a mistake, aren't hitting frequency targets, or aren't getting the outcomes you want, how do you respond? Do you view that data as a helpful learning moment and provide one-on-one coaching to help your team members improve? Or do you call it out publicly, express frustration, and try to shame people into doing a better job?

EOS TIP: THE ISSUES SOLVING TRACK (IDS)

The two-part Meeting Pulse and Weekly Scorecards (see EOS Tips on pages 97 and 102) are EOS Tools that make it easier to lead and manage well, and to strengthen your company's Process Component. There's a third EOS Tool, the Issues Solving Track, that is essential as you work to get these core processes followed by all.

The Issues Solving Track is something of a mini-process for solving issues effectively. It improves a team's ability to identify and resolve issues as they arise rather than letting them linger for days, weeks, sometimes even years. Here's how it works, in the context of strengthening your Process Component.

When a Scorecard number is off track during your weekly Level 10 Meeting, you'll "drop it down" to the Issues List. During the section of the meeting agenda set aside for solving issues, you'll prioritize the one, two, and three most important issues to solve today. Because hitting weekly, activities-based numbers is often the key to getting great results, teams often prioritize off-track Scorecard numbers first.

Once you've prioritized, simply focus on issue number one and "IDS" it. The *I* in IDS stands for *Identify*. In other words, what is the *real* issue? It's not unusual for a symptom to land on your Issues List. In fact, an underperforming sales team might be the symptom of several different real issues or *root causes*. Treating symptoms is a temporary fix. Instead, let's figure out what root cause we really need to resolve, and make this issue go away forever.

Once the root cause is clear, we move to *D* and *Discuss* the issue briefly. People say what needs to be said once, and only once, because more than once is politicking. The final step is *S*, because we then *Solve* the issue by agreeing on a plan of attack that we believe will resolve it for the long-term and greater good. *Solve* typically requires a decision and an agreement to take action.

Having your core processes documented, simplified, and followed by all will help improve your ability to *Identify* the root causes of your issues and *Solve* them forever. Likewise, being in a regular Meeting Pulse and using IDS to solve issues will help strengthen your company's Process Component more quickly and effectively.

When every member of your team understands the reasons for change and feels valued and supported on their journey, permanent change is possible. That won't happen without your full commitment to lead and manage well yourself, and to help every manager, supervisor, or team lead in your company do the same. If you'd like to learn more about how to lead and manage well, consider reading *How to Be a Great Boss* by our colleagues Gino Wickman and René Boer.

Jere Simpson is the founder and Visionary of Kitewire, a software company that helps businesses and institutions manage mobile devices. He explains the value of the *Manage* step in the FBA Checklist by sharing this story:

"About two years in, our business stalled at $4M. I would be so frustrated as to why we couldn't predict anything. Ultimately, I realized it was because we weren't following processes and we were reauthoring our approach each time. Our company had a culture of winging it, and I decided to embrace a culture of discipline. We documented our processes and worked on getting them followed by the twenty people on our team.

"This was a *huge* culture shift that required a major gut check, because we shifted our focus from growth to consistent execution. That first year, in fact, we experienced a dip in revenue down to $3.2M—which was significant for us. However, once we changed the culture, we grew *80 percent* each year for three years in a row." Ten years later, the company is widely recognized as an industry leader with delighted customers and steady, profitable growth. That success, a great leadership team, and a strong Process Component gave Jere the leverage to successfully sell his business and pursue other passions—including his next scalable business idea!

- **Update** each process regularly, at least once per year. This is essential for two reasons. First, it creates a culture of regular improvement. Your first effort helped reduce waste, inefficiencies, inconsistencies, and mistakes. Now it's time to build on that firm foundation. Can you further simplify the process?

Can you automate, streamline, or eliminate steps? Our clients find that asking these questions annually ensures their Process Component remains strong over time.

> It is not the strongest of the species that survives,
> not the most intelligent that survives. It is the
> one that is most adaptable to change.
> **—Charles Darwin**

The second reason for updating your processes is, quite simply, survival. Time stands still for no company. As the story about Uber's impact on taxi companies illustrates, those who fail to adapt will perish. Celebrate your accomplishments, for certain. However, feeling great about the way things work today doesn't mean that your approach will be the simplest and best way to operate tomorrow. Your industry is changing, your customers' needs are changing, technology is changing, and your business should be changing as well. Updating your core processes at least once per year is a habit that will help you respond to and even anticipate those changes. You will survive and thrive, leaving competitors who don't adapt in your wake.

We've seen clients manage the update step of the FBA Checklist in several ways, but all of them involve clear accountability—and a calendar. First, make sure one member of your leadership team owns each process. As mentioned earlier, the appropriate choice for this assignment is often clear as it is tied to their role on the accountability chart. When you have one core process that spans multiple major functions (customer service, for example), pick a leader who will take responsibility for updating that process at least annually.

One growing software company helps lenders predict when a borrower is likely to be ready for a loan. Because they were hiring five to ten people per month, keeping processes up to date and easy to use became critical. They found a technology platform that not only simplified and centralized the processes but also reminded them to review and update their processes regularly. Whenever a member of the leadership team made a change, the software prompted employees to revisit the process for additional training. This approach made the employees more confident in the quality of their work, and the leaders more confident in the company's ability to serve its customers consistently well and continue to grow.

Jere Simpson of Kitewire used this step in the FBA Checklist to make a radical change in the company's people process. He was inspired by superstar basketball player LeBron James, who attributes his longevity at the top of his sport to the significant time he devotes to mental and physical recovery. Simpson realized with his company's improved performance and accomplished leadership team, he could institute a four-day work week. Not only did that adjustment help the team attract and retain great talent, he found that performance improved quarter over quarter. Furthermore, the move made it possible for Jere and other team members to spend more quality time with their young families.

Once the owners of each process have been identified, spread responsibility for updating core processes throughout the year. Most of our clients do this on a quarterly basis because that's how frequently they establish Rocks (the 90-day business priorities described on page 69). One EOS client shared this simple table, with each leader owning several processes because they are reviewed during different quarters of the year:

Owner	Process	When
Sharon	Marketing	Q2
	Sales	Q3
	Account Management	Q1
Carlos	Engineering	Q4
	Supply Chain	Q1
	Production	Q2
Simon	Accounting	Q2
	HR	Q3
	IT	Q4
Rachel	Running the Business	Q3
	M&A	Q1

With accountability clearly established, leaders in a company running on EOS simply set Rocks in the appropriate quarter to review and update their core process. This approach can be plugged into whatever approach your company takes to set priorities and drive accountability for completing them. If you don't have a way of operating like that, consider adopting a business operating process. We don't believe *every* business needs to run on EOS, but we do know that you cannot run a great business on multiple operating systems. You must choose one.

Once you've prioritized updating a process, the ideal approach is very much like the steps you first used to document and simplify the core process:

1. Observe
2. Evaluate
3. Revise the process
4. Restart the FBA Checklist
   - Retrain everyone
   - Revise measurements, as necessary
   - Manage well, focusing on the steps or substeps that changed

If you do that once per year with each process, you'll have a living, breathing blueprint for consistent excellence in your business. You'll see opportunities for improvement and anticipate the ever-changing needs of your customers before your competitors do. You'll also take advantage of technology, eliminate waste, and manage change better than they do. You'll get better, smarter, faster—quarter in and quarter out. You'll not only be the opposite of obsolete, you'll be unstoppable!

That's the power of the FBA Checklist, not to mention this whole approach to driving discipline, consistency, and continuous improvement into your business. When your core processes are documented, simplified, and followed by all (FBA), you'll be able to scale your business to any size you choose. You'll also be free to lead, create, and innovate while living your ideal life.

SECTION III

ACT

THE PROCESS! PROCESS

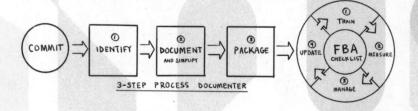

CHAPTER 6

· · · · · · · · · · · · · ·

YOUR ACTION PLAN

Until now, we've been preparing you for the journey ahead. Now it's time to take action, and chapter 6 will help you do that with clarity and confidence. As we mentioned at the outset, the workflow visual represents both a summary of what you've just learned and a proven, step-by-step approach to strengthening your organization's Process Component. In other words, it's the "*Process!* Process." Here's how you can use it to customize your plan, take action, and get results.

COMMIT

Commitment: It separates doers from dreamers.
—John Maxwell

In chapter 1, we explored the many ways entrepreneurs and business leaders may need to adjust their mindset to see the value of process. Chapter 2 detailed the many benefits of a strong Process Component and the costs of a weak one. In chapters 3 through 5 we taught you how to document, simplify, and get your core processes followed by all by using the 3-Step Process Documenter and the FBA Checklist. While we're thrilled that any doubts you may have had didn't prevent you from reading on, we've not made a positive impact on your business or your life if we don't help you take action. To do that well, you must commit.

Strengthening your Process Component is simple, but not always easy. You will encounter resistance, some of it from the person looking back at you in the mirror every morning. Ali Nasser, founder and CEO of AltruVista, a wealth management firm, described his feelings early on by saying, "Until I fully embraced the power of this work, it felt like I was being hit with the process stick." Another resisted process because he thought it was "boring," until he realized what a positive impact it would have on his company's ability to evolve and innovate.

Expect people from every level of your organization to hold back, push back, or act out. Resistance to change is normal—especially when that change involves rigor, discipline, and accountability. If only it were possible to get consistently exceptional results *without* those things!

That's why you must believe in the power of this work with firm resolve. When you're fully committed, it's easier to lean into and even appreciate the inevitable challenges and obstacles you encounter. You will have the confidence to encourage people to speak up and share their thoughts and emotions. You'll appreciate that a team member expressing concerns is engaging in the journey, passionately if not always positively.

When that happens, listen carefully to what people are saying. Seek to truly understand where they're coming from, and why they feel so strongly. Avoid cutting off or dismissing these legitimate concerns. As Patrick Lencioni explained in *The Five Dysfunctions of a Team*, people can typically support a decision or initiative they originally disagreed with, but only when they feel heard.

Be vulnerable and willing to share your own concerns and misgivings. Explain what you've learned that changed your mind. Frankly, we wrote this book to help you and your fellow leaders embrace something that many entrepreneurial leaders reject out of hand. If your teammates are struggling to commit, share this book with them. If a member of your team is falling prey to common myths, ask them to read chapter 1. Those who don't understand the value of this work can read chapter 2. And chapters 3 through 5 are for those ready and willing to learn how to do it. If anyone remains reluctant or unsure, make it absolutely clear that you intend to move forward with this initiative, and that you need their full support. Ask for everyone's commitment to the journey ahead, and get a verbal, heartfelt "yes." If you have any doubt about the sincerity of that commitment, ask again. False harmony is more dangerous than actual dissension.

COMPLETE THE 3-STEP PROCESS DOCUMENTER

The opposite of discipline is actually laziness.

—Seth Godin

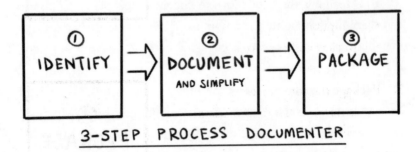

3-STEP PROCESS DOCUMENTER

Once you are firmly committed, you can quit discussing, debating and procrastinating and start *doing*. Using the 3-Step Process Documenter detailed in chapter 3, simply gather your team and get started. Here's a high-level summary of the major steps in this process:

1. **Identify** your handful of core processes

   - Meet with your leadership team
   - Clearly define *handful of core processes*
   - Brainstorm, compile, and *keep, kill, combine*
   - Name each process
   - Create a table of contents for your core process manual

2. **Document** and **Simplify** each
   process
   - Create a plan
   - Observe
   - Evaluate
   - Document
   - Simplify
   - Review and approve

3. **Package** the core processes
   - Determine the right medium/format
   - Gather, organize, package, or store them
   - Name it (for example, *The ABC Company Way*)
   - Make them easy to find and use

For most companies, this takes about twelve months (give or take a quarter). Set a realistic timeline, stay focused, and keep moving forward. If you get stuck or encounter resistance, use the tools described in section I, *Commit*, and section II, chapter 5, *The FBA Checklist*, and press on. As you'll soon see, we'll be updating and improving each process regularly.

COMPLETE THE FBA CHECKLIST

> You do not rise to the level of your goals,
> you fall to the level of your systems.
> **—James Clear, *Power of Habit***

Your packaged core process manual (in whatever format) is a blueprint for a better future, one in which you're consistently getting the results you want such as growth, profit, great team members, happy employees, and ultimately, freedom. The FBA Checklist turns that blueprint into a system, one in which your core processes are followed by all.

1. **Train**
   - Everyone who does one or more steps
   - Pick the right training method
   - Encourage candid dialog, even pushback
   - Verify understanding and commitment
   - Repeat yourself often (as necessary)

2. **Measure**
   - Compliance—are we doing it right?
   - Frequency—are we doing it often enough to get the desired results?

- Outcome—are we getting the result we want?
- Determine who, how, and where
- Set goals

3. **Manage** (or LMA)
    - LMA (lead and manage in a way that drives accountability)
    - Support team members as behaviors change
    - Reward and recognize great results

4. **Update**
    - As needed (at least annually)
    - Engage the team
    - Streamline, automate, simplify
    - Repeat checklist item 1, *Train*
    - Adjust the way you *Measure* and *Manage*, as needed

One important disclaimer: Getting your core processes followed by using the checklist does not mean everyone will always follow the process and never make a mistake. It simply means you have built a machine to drive accountability for following processes, getting results, and reacting more quickly and definitively when mistakes are made or goals are not achieved. And, remember, as we shared in the *Update* section, your work here is never done. As the world evolves, your organization, its processes, and its people will evolve with it—faster and better than the competition.

CHAPTER 7

· · · · · · · · · · · · ·

OVERCOMING CHALLENGES

No matter how well you execute the steps we've laid out above, you're likely to encounter obstacles along the way. After all, we assume that you lead and manage people—not robots. Some of the most common challenges we've seen other leaders face are listed below, along with ways you can overcome them.

- **Lack of Passion.** Even if you begin this project with the right mindset, your commitment may fade periodically or over time. You may also encounter members of your team who just can't get excited about strengthening your Process Component. This obstacle is common . . . and dangerous. Entrepreneurs and innovative leaders often struggle or flat out abandon projects for which they have little to no passion. Don't be afraid to ask your leadership team for help—they may be the ones who are excited about the project right now and you can borrow their energy.

Knowing this is likely to happen before you get started will help you take steps to either prevent it or respond more quickly when people lose energy for this project. Get your mindset right from the beginning (see section I, *Commit*) and keep coming back to *why* this work is important. Remind your team that you're investing in process to get consistently better results and achieve the company's vision. Keep your people focused on truths (not myths) and the many benefits of strengthening your Process Component. That will help all of you stay positive and agree that driving change is a solid investment in the future of your business.

Another way to keep enthusiasm high is to plan for early wins. When prioritizing which core process(es) you're going to tackle first, remember that *less is more*. It's better to succeed with one process than to tackle five at once and never complete any of them. Also, consider picking the process or processes that will have an immediate, positive impact. What's causing the most pain in your organization right now? Or, where can we succeed most quickly in a measurable way? One or two easy or important wins will boost energy for the rest of your journey.

If passion *does* begin to fade, speak up. When those feelings and worries are ignored or unspoken, they will fester and spread. As a result, the project may blow up or die on the vine. Whether on your own or with the help of your team, trust the process and keep moving forward. As Sir Winston Churchill said, "If you're going through Hell, keep going." Strengthen your resolve, reignite your passion, and get this important project back on track.

- **Lack of Expertise.** As you can see, this is a simple, practical approach that does not require deep, specific process expertise. It does require passion, knowledge of your business, and a strong desire to consistently execute and regularly improve. You also need a team that's willing to do the work.

   Of course, experience with process *is* an asset. Having at least one member of your leadership team who's done prior work driving consistent execution with process will help you. Having someone who's been at a company with a strong Process Component is like having the cover of a jigsaw puzzle box to guide you on this journey. It's helpful to know what "done" looks like. It also means when you encounter an obstacle, someone on the team can say with authority, "Here are a few ways we could solve this problem." Without that real-world experience in the room, team members may spend more time dealing in conjecture and opinions instead of experience.

   Don't let this slow you down or grind the project to a halt. We've seen teams with no prior process experience strengthen the heck out of their Process Component. If you lack expertise, like other businesses, you may not get everything exactly right the first time—just keep moving. Perfect is the enemy of progress. If you feel you are permanently stuck or want to move faster, the lack-of-expertise challenge can be solved one of three ways:

1. **Develop the knowledge and skills of your existing team.** Invest time or money in learning about process. Read books, attend seminars, or engage with process experts in your industry that are willing to share their experience with you.

2. **Find or hire someone with relevant experience.** You may have an unidentified process expert in your business who can participate alongside the leadership team in driving this project forward. Several of the companies discussed in this book identified the "process champion" in their company who contributed significantly to the success of their process goals. If your company has not already identified this person, consider adding "process expertise" as a required quality of your next key hire. Rigor and discipline for process is going to become more important as your company grows—and not just in operations. It's not unusual to find experienced leaders with process expertise in other disciplines, such as finance, HR, sales, and marketing.

3. **Partner with a process firm or expert.** The word *partner* is really important here. You do not want to hire someone to do all the heavy lifting for you. Remember: your team needs to own it. So, find a person or company with the

experience and bandwidth to help your team do better work. Search "process consulting" or "business process management" and you'll find hundreds of firms and individuals with deep process expertise available to help you. Be explicit about the role you want them to play and select one whose style and approach is a good fit for your team.

- **Love of Complexity or Perfection.** If you or other members of your team struggle with simplicity or incremental progress, this initiative may stall in the "ready, aim, aim, aim" mode. Remember: we're focused on progress, not perfection.

  Start with the basics, the 20 percent of the work that gets you 80 percent of the results. Get those core processes as close to "done" as you can at the outset, then refine, update, and improve these processes over time. If you believe that only a detailed, five-hundred-page SOP manual will do, start with this simple approach and use it as an outline for your more detailed process manual of the future. Otherwise, you may be doing *lots and lots* of work without ever making a positive impact in the business. In our experience, that's a luxury most entrepreneurial companies simply do not have.

- **Overreliance on Technology.** Some companies and leaders look to technology as a way to strengthen their Process Component. They acquire a new ERP hoping to standardize business operating processes, or a new CRM to more consistently market, sell to, and serve customers. Some providers of these products actually tout their ability to do just that. It *is* true that systems, software, and tech platforms can help. However, starting with and relying on technology is letting the tail wag the dog.

Use technology to streamline, standardize, and consistently execute *your* business' best practices. All reputable technology firms agree. In fact, gathering a company's core processes is typically one of the first steps in an ERP or CRM implementation project. So please, start by getting your core processes documented, simplified, and followed by all using the approach laid out in this book. Once you've done that, your technology implementation will move faster and get better results.

Skip that important first step at your own peril. A successful company running on EOS made that mistake, and their Visionary was gracious enough to share the story. At significant expense, the firm decided to adopt a new ERP from an industry-leading firm whose clients include many of the Global Fortune 500. The design and implementation project consumed a tremendous amount of time at all levels of the organization.

After fifteen months and a failed launch, the leadership team made the tough decision to scrap the new software system. They reinstalled their legacy system, stabilized operations, and turned their attention to strengthening the company's Process Component. Two years later, the company reaped the rewards of their work and broke through the ceiling. Their revenue is growing steadily, profit margin has increased materially, and their functional and far less expensive ERP is working well.

- **Lack of Leadership.** This advice may hit a little close to home, but managing change of this magnitude requires strong and consistent leadership and management. Do you and your leadership team truly *own* this initiative? Have you helped everyone understand *why* you're doing it and made it clear that allowing everyone to do things their own way is not an option? Have you stayed engaged and committed from the start? Are you involving everyone in the organization and truly listening to their questions, concerns, and feedback? Have you driven accountability for learning and following these processes and consistently hitting numbers?

If the answer to any of these questions is *no*, then, like many of the leaders in our companies realized later than they would have liked, you may be the reason you're stuck. Convert all those answers to a *yes* and you'll get unstuck.

- **No/Poor Training.** Far too many process improvement initiatives fail because only documenting and simplifying the processes will not change the way people do their jobs. It's the training—and then reinforcement with measurables and management—that will create new habits and consistently better results. Unfortunately, many busy leaders and managers struggle to find the time to develop, deliver, and reinforce that crucial training.

  Your core processes create the foundation for a world-class onboarding, training, and development program. Use them! Set aside time to develop an initial training program that walks all employees, new and seasoned, through the new process. Make it interactive, collaborative, and (gasp!) even fun. We have learned that people need to hear things seven times to hear them for the first time, so be prepared to repeat training until the new way has become "the way we do things around here."

- **No/Poor Measurement.** Measuring compliance, frequency, and outcomes provides evidence that the process you created and the training you conducted has begun to move the needle. If you're not measuring those things regularly (we recommend weekly), your employees and managers may quickly revert to old habits. We see two types of obstacles to effective measurement: one is tactical, and the other is cultural.

  The *tactical* challenge is figuring out what to measure and how to measure it. Which of the major steps in our core process is most important to measure? Once we make that decision, should we measure compliance, frequency, or outcome for this step? Finally, *how* are we going to measure that? If you're stuck here, these are the right questions to be asking and answering. We'd simply urge you to follow one of the 10 Commandments of Solving Issues from the book *Traction*: "Thou shalt take a shot."

  Pick a major step, choose compliance, frequency, or outcome, and figure out the simplest, best way to measure it right now. You don't need the latest and greatest software to measure leads, opportunities, errors, waste, or on-time delivery. Some of the most effective measurement methods have involved whiteboards or notepads and tick marks. Data from the latest software applications may be better, but don't let the lack of automation prevent you from getting started. Once you decide what to measure and how to measure it, set a goal. Look at the number every day, week, or month and when it's off track, work with your team to understand why and get it back on track.

  The *cultural* challenge is convincing your team to accept and even embrace the value of having a number that they are accountable for hitting. Many employees believe that their boss is tracking measurables to catch them making mistakes or not working hard enough. Help them understand that these numbers are actually *their* tools, designed to help them perform at a consistently high level. Clear goals for compliance, frequency, and outcomes define success—allowing any employee who wants to be successful to know instantly what's working and what's not. Those who are naturally accountable will *love* the clarity that provides. Those who would prefer *not* to be accountable will resist and may leave. And that brings us to our next obstacle.

- **Avoidance of Accountability.** The success of any organization is directly proportional to the accountability of its people. When leaders, managers, and individual contributors are accountable for getting results, an organization thrives. When hitting numbers, completing priorities, serving customers and employees well, and resolving issues is somebody else's job, an organization is doomed to fail. This principle also applies to strengthening your Process Component—accountability is key.

For one leader, strengthening his company's Process Component was the key to confronting that reality head on. "For years," the CEO of this second-generation family business confessed, "I would sit in meetings and blame lack of processes for our stalled growth and low profitability.

"Once we documented our processes and trained everyone," he continued, "I was forced to address the fact that lack of documentation wasn't the problem. What held us back was people refusing to *follow* the process. Despite having built and implemented these tools at the company level, people were independently using their own scorecard, their own operating system, and their own processes. A lot of long-time employees had habits that had to be broken. When we got everyone to follow our core processes, the business became a well-oiled machine. Yes, it was hard work and, yes, it was worth the effort."

If your employees don't want to change or won't work hard to keep their numbers on track, you'll quickly go back to the old way of doing things. If your leaders and managers won't drive accountability for changing behaviors and executing with rigor and discipline, this initiative will fail. If there are no consequences for not following the process or not getting the desired results, you'll never achieve your business' potential on a consistent basis.

We get what we tolerate. If you embark on this journey, please be *personally* accountable for leading the change you seek. Expect accountability from your leaders, managers, and team members. You can do this with compassion and understanding, but you must be clear and firm. Create an environment where accountable people are recognized, rewarded, and celebrated. One in which the people unwilling or unable to change are coached and supported until they either get on board or leave. Either way, your company will be stronger.

One leader acknowledged that her team members really struggled with accountability for changing habits. "People were confused, scared, and angry," she said. "We argued. We cried. We even fought. Some people left on their own. Others were asked to leave. It was hard, but it was worth it. Our culture is better today. Our people are better at what they do, happier, and fully accountable. Our leaders and managers are more effective, and we love coming to work every day. I wouldn't change a thing."

- **"Kind of" Syndrome.** Without question, this is the number one obstacle for well-intentioned leadership teams struggling to strengthen their Process Component. If you know what to do and how to do it but are not yet getting the results you want, it may be that "kind of" is killing you. We named the syndrome based on dozens of client interactions, all of which feel eerily similar. They all go something like this:

Us: Are you consistently getting the results you want?

Client: No.

Us: How strong is your Process Component?

Client: Maybe 55 percent out of 100.

Us: Are your core processes documented, simplified, and followed by all?

Client: Hmm . . . kind of?

Us: Wait, kind of? Let me be more specific: Did the team identify your handful of core processes and agree with what they are and what you're going to call them forever?

Client: Well, not exactly . . .

Us (more urgently): Okay, well did you document and simplify each core process, then work with the leadership team to get 100 percent approval and alignment that this is the right way to do that process?

Client: Gosh . . . probably not 100%.

Us (turning a subtle shade of crimson): Okay, well, did you train everyone who performs even one step in the process?

Client: Sort of?

And this goes on and on and on.

If we're not being clear, this "kind of" back and forth is excruciatingly frustrating. These teams know what needs to be done, they've got the tools to do the work, yet they remain stuck and frustrated. This work is about clarifying and simplifying the way things get done every day. We're very specific about how to do that, and "kind of" or "sort of" doing the work just will not produce the results you want. In fact, "kind of" documenting, simplifying, and getting your core processes followed by all may be worse than not doing it at all! You'll spend precious time going through the motions, and when in the end nothing changes, your team will lose confidence in the power of process. That's why, in our humble opinion, "kind of" will *kill you*!

We've been fortunate to support teams that overcome these obstacles by following the steps outlined in this book. Stay consistent, return to the fundamentals outlined in this book, and refer to the templates provided in the next section. In short, trust the *Process!* Process.

. . . .

CHAPTER 8

TEMPLATES AND RESOURCES

COMMIT – ADOPTING THE RIGHT MINDSET

PROCESS! MINDSET QUESTIONNAIRE

Rate each statement on a scale of 1–10 with 1 = "strongly disagree" and 10 = "strongly agree."

1. My passion and enthusiasm for this business is high.	
2. The business consistently produces the results I want.	
3. I believe process will have a powerful, positive impact on my business.	
4. Our leadership team believes process will have a powerful, positive impact on our business.	
5. I am experienced and knowledgeable when it comes to process.	
6. Our leadership team is experienced and knowledgeable when it comes to process.	
7. Our entire organization will be excited about instilling rigor and discipline for process.	
8. Process is in my nature.	
9. Process will take some time, but it will be worth it.	
10. Process will create freedom for me.	
Total	

Scoring Key:

10–40   Your mindset is resistant. Read (or reread) *Process!* and consider the resources listed below.

41–80   Your mindset is not fully committed, review section I.

81–100   Your mindset is right; your chances of success are high.

ADDITIONAL RESOURCES TO IMPROVE YOUR MINDSET

- **Atomic Habits**, James Clear
- **The EOS Life**, Gino Wickman
- **Checklist Manifesto**, Atul Gawande
- **The Goal**, Eli Goldratt

COMMIT – UNDERSTANDING *WHY* PROCESS IS IMPORTANT

THINKING AND DISCUSSION EXERCISES

For each of these *benefits* of a strong Process Component, list some specific, measurable ways your company would be impacted by this work:

Growing faster _____

_____

Attracting and retaining talent _____

_____

Creating a culture of excellence _____

_____

Making customers happier _____

_____

Having more time _____

_____

Making more money _____

_____

Increasing the value of my company _____

_____

Living a better life _____

_____

Which of those specific benefits do you find most compelling? Why?

_____

_____

_____

_____

_____

_____

_____

_____

_____

_____

_____

_____

_____

_____

_____

_____

_____

_____

_____

_____

_____

For each of these costs of a weak Process Component, list some specific, measurable ways your company would be impacted by this work:

Trouble finding and keeping great people _____

_____

Stalled business growth _____

_____

Business fails to innovate _____

_____

Business vulnerable to extinction _____

_____

Which of those specific risks or costs do you find most concerning? Why?

_____

_____

_____

_____

_____

_____

_____

_____

_____

Combine the specific benefits and costs above to calculate the potential ROI of strengthening your Process Component:

_____

_____

_____

_____

_____

_____

_____

_____

_____

_____

_____

_____

_____

_____

_____

_____

_____

_____

THE 3-STEP PROCESS DOCUMENTER—STEP 1

IDENTIFY	
Who:	Leadership Team
Facilitated By:	Process Champion
What:	Identify your handful of core processes
Summary:	Leadership Team meets to select and name its handful of core processes
Time:	One hour
Final Product:	Table of contents for company's "process manual"

MAJOR STEPS

- Identify the Process Champion (Leader with the skill/determination to drive this project)
- Schedule a 60-minute meeting
- Create the proper context
- Illustrate a list of (generic) core processes
- Each leader makes his/her/their own list
- Compile complete list on whiteboard
- Consolidate list with "Keep, Kill, Combine" until Leadership Team agrees on a handful (5–12)
- Leadership Team agrees on a name for each core process
- Process Champion turns the list into a table of contents for the future process manual, drive, or library

Step 1: Identify your handful of core processes. What are the five to twelve most important, repetitive processes that make your company uniquely valuable?

_____

_____

_____

_____

_____

_____

_____

_____

_____

_____

_____

_____

_____

_____

_____

_____

THE 3-STEP PROCESS DOCUMENTER—STEP 2

DOCUMENT AND SIMPLIFY	
Who:	Leadership Team Members
Facilitated By:	N/A
What:	Document and Simplify
Summary:	Each Leadership Team Member observes, outlines, and simplifies 20% of the major steps that achieve 80% of the results
Time:	90 days for 1–3 processes per person
Result:	A draft core process in 1–5 page document
Tools:	3-Step Process Documenter Sample HR process Getting What You Want See examples, page 154–156

MAJOR STEPS

- Leadership Team agrees on a plan:
  - Format
  - Due date
- Prioritize and schedule each process
- Identify an owner for each process
- One process at a time:
  - Observe the process as it's done today
  - Ask questions and learn
  - Evaluate; look for ways to simplify
  - Draft a simplified core process
  - Get Leadership Team approval

Step 2: Document and Simplify

Plan

_____

_____

_____

_____

_____

_____

_____

_____

_____

_____

_____

_____

_____

_____

_____

_____

_____

_____

Observe

Process Name _____

Observer _____

Date _____

Notes

_____

_____

_____

_____

_____

_____

_____

_____

_____

_____

_____

_____

_____

_____

_____

_____

_____

_____

_____

Evaluate

Process Name _____

Observer _____

Date _____

What works well?

_____

_____

_____

_____

_____

_____

_____

What's not working?

_____

_____

_____

_____

_____

_____

_____

Draft: Owner: _____ Due Date: _____

Approve: Date: _____

THE 3-STEP PROCESS DOCUMENTER™

Step 1 - Identify

- Identify your handful of core processes
- Make a list (HR, Marketing, Sales, Several Operations, Accounting, Customer Service/Retention, etc.)
- Give each of them a name, with everyone agreeing to use that name

Step 2 - Document

- One at a time, record the major steps in each core process:
  - Favor a linear/chronological approach
  - Each major step should be supported by 1-5 sub-points defining the who/what/where/ when/how
  - Keep it simple (the 20/80 approach) Each core process should be fully documented in 1-5 pages
- Review and approve each core process – every member of the leadership team must agree *this* is the right way to do it every time
- Repeat this step for every core process

The
ABC
Way

Step 3 - Package

- Combine each documented and simplified core process into a binder, online folder or other accessible, easy-to-find package
- Turn your list of core processes (from Step 1) into your table of contents
- Give it a name. The ABC Way, Franchise Model, Operating Model, SOP, Circle of Life, etc.

THE H/R PROCESS

The Search
- Define role/job description/salary (the seat in the Accountability Chart™)
- Decide search medium
- Begin search
- E-mail blast to sphere/peers

Interviewing
- Screen résumés
- Initial interview/profiling tools
- 2nd interview
- Check references
- CEO interview

Hiring
- 8-hour on-the-job trial
- Decision
- 90-day trial

Orientation
- H/R policy/review employee manual
- Benefits review/forms
- Job training
- CEO orientation (company story/core ideology)

Quarterly Conversations
- What's working, what's not?
- Review the 5-5-5™/People Analyzer™ (RPRS)
- Review LMA questionnaires
- Delegate and elevate opportunities
- Update Accountability Chart if necessary

Annual Reviews
- Manager fills out People Analyzer, including GWC™ in preparation for the review
- Document the review and have it signed by all parties
- File the review with the H/R department

Termination
- 3-strike system (30-30-30)
- Terminate upon 3rd strike
- Contact legal counsel
- Meet with employee/have H/R present
- Exit interview
- Document termination and have it signed by all parties

www.eosworldwide.com   © 2003–2022 EOS. All Rights Reserved.

GETTING WHAT YOU WANT

What are the end results you are hoping to achieve? What do you really want? This tool will help you define the steps you will need to take to get what you want and the measurables for tracking those procedural steps or activities.

Example 1

	Add Target Prospect to List	Make Contacts	First Meeting
	8 / WK	4 / WK	2 / WK

Instructions: State the desired end result, in the box at the far right. In the boxes to the left, define the activities leading to the end result including the measurables that specify how much or to what level each activity needs to be completed. Further develop your process with the 3-Step Process Documenter™, circle key measurables and add them to your Scorecard, or define the critical steps to achieve your Rock.

What Do You Want?

Needs Assessment	Create Proposal	Present Proposal	1 New Client/MO
1 / WK	2 / MO	2 / MO	

What Do You Want?

What Do You Want?

Inbound Service Call Process

Objective: Define the decisions and actions of the customer service representative (CSR) to assure that each customer inquiry and request for service is addressed our company way.

Who: Customer Service Representative

1. Caller Outreach
   - Live Answer: Inquiry Received
   - Non-Live Answer: Voicemail, Web, Emails, Follow-Up
2. Identify Caller's Needs
   - Appointment Related: New, Return, Reschedule, Cancel
   - Non-Appointment Related: Warranty, Other Dept, Third-Party Solicitation
3. Capture Customer Information
4. Follow Our Process
   - Address Questions
   - Address Objections
5. Schedule Appt or Refer to Department
6. Complete Call
7. Review and Update Information
   - Communicate to Everyone Who Needs to Know
   - Follow Process for Customer, Software, Calendar Communications

SAMPLE FORMATS

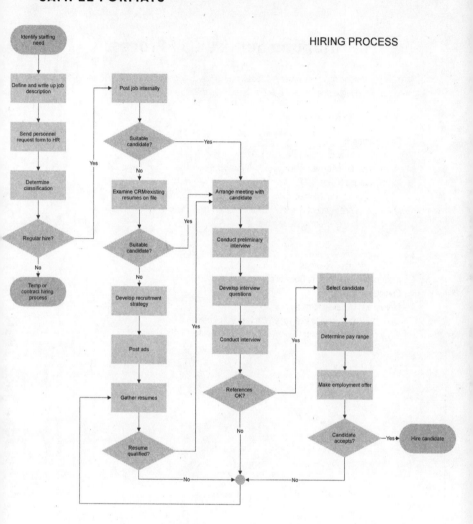

HIRING PROCESS

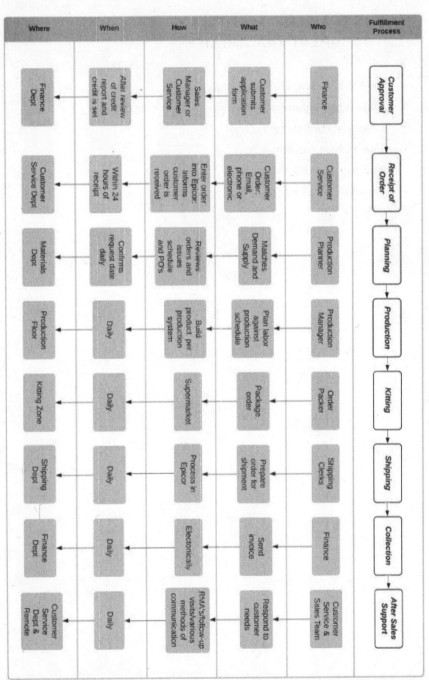

CUSTOMER FULFILLMENT CORE PROCESS

Fulfillment Process	Who	What	How	When	Where
Customer Approval	Finance	Customer submits application form	Sales Manager or Customer Service	After review of credit report and credit is set	Finance Dept
Receipt of Order	Customer Service	Customer Order, Email, phone or electronic	Enter order into Epicor. Informs customer order is received	Within 24 hours of receipt	Customer Service Dept
Planning	Production Planner	Matches Demand and Supply	Reviews orders and issues schedule and PO's	Confirms request date daily	Materials Dept
Production	Production Manager	Plan labor against production schedule	Build product per production system	Daily	Production Floor
Kitting	Order Packer	Package order	Supermarket	Daily	Kitting Zone
Shipping	Shipping Clerks	Prepare order for shipment	Process in Epicor	Daily	Shipping Dept
Collection	Finance	Send invoice	Electronically	Daily	Finance Dept
After Sales Support	Customer Service & Sales Team	Respond to customer needs	RMA's/follow-up visits/various methods of communication	Daily	Customer Service Dept & Remote

ADDITIONAL RESOURCES TO HELP
YOU DOCUMENT AND SIMPLIFY

- **EOS Worldwide**, EOSOne.com
- **Object Management Group**, bpmn.org or omg.org
- **Creately**, creately.com
- **Lucid Chart**, lucidchart.com
- **Monday**, monday.com
- **Smart Draw**, smartdraw.com

THE 3-STEP PROCESS DOCUMENTER—STEP 3

PACKAGE	
Who:	Leadership Team
Facilitated By:	Process Champion or Team Leader
What:	Decide how to package core processes so they are easy to find and use
Summary:	Consider the who, what, where, when, and how for each process; select the platform and format that will make each process easy to find and use.
Time:	Research: 1–3 months; Decision: 1 hour
Result:	See Examples, pages 88–89, 151, 154–156
Tools:	Various, depends on approach selected

MAJOR STEPS

- Research platforms and formats
- Share with Leadership Team
- Meet for 1 hour:
  - Discuss the who, what, when, where, and how for each process
  - Identify the platforms/formats that would work best
  - IDS until the team decides on a platform/format
  - Start the "manual" with your table of contents from step 1
- For each process:
  - Document and simplify in the agreed-upon format
  - Package as processes are completed
  - Ensure each process is simple, clear, easy to find, and easy to use

ADDITIONAL RESOURCES TO HELP YOU *PACKAGE*

- **Asana**, asana.com
- **Playbook Builder**, teamplaybookbuilder.com
- **Process Street**, process.st
- **Trainual**, trainual.com
- **Whale**, usewhale.io

FBA CHECKLIST—STEP 1

TRAIN	
Who:	Leadership Team
Facilitated By:	Team Leader or Process Champion
What:	Train everyone who performs one or more steps in the process
Summary:	For each process, identify participants and select the right approach. Plan, prepare for, and complete training. Validate understanding and a desire to change behaviors.
Time:	One week to several months
Result:	Every employee understands the new process and is willing to adopt it as a new way of operating
Tools:	Documented, simplified core processes and appropriate training venue, guides, and tools

MAJOR STEPS

- Identify people who perform one or more steps in the process
- Determine the best approach to training (classroom, one-on-one, virtual, etc.)
- Schedule and prepare (venue, guides, tools, instructors, etc.)
- Complete training event(s). Encourage active participation, suggestions, even pushback
- Validate understanding and commitment

ADDITIONAL RESOURCES TO HELP YOU *TRAIN*

- **Telling Ain't Training**, Harold D. Stolovitch and Erica J. Keeps
- **The Art and Science of Training**, Elaine Biech
- **The Six Disciplines of Breakthrough Learning**, Roy V.H. Pollock, Andy Jefferson, and Calhoun W. Wick
- **Training Reinforcement**, Anthonie Wurth

FBA CHECKLIST—STEP 2

MEASURE	
Who:	Leaders and managers whose people perform steps in the process
Facilitated By:	Process Champion or Individual Process Owner
What:	Reinforce training and adoption by implementing measurement of major steps in each process
Summary:	For each process, decide how to measure major steps for compliance, frequency, or outcome. Implement those measurables/metrics and use them to change behaviors and improve results.
Time:	One to three months, ongoing
Result:	People adopt the new process, new habits are formed, results improve.
Tools:	Scorecards or dashboards. Tools to gather and report the data.

STEPS

- Identify which steps to measure
- Decide whether to measure compliance (doing it right), frequency (doing it often enough) or outcomes (getting the desired result)
- Determine how best to gather the data
- Determine how best to report the data
- Review regularly (we recommend weekly) with the people using the process
- Refine/improve as necessary

COMPANY SCORECARD EXAMPLE

Who	Measurable	Goal	1	2	3	4	5	6	7	8	9	10	11	12	13
									Weeks						
Sue	New leads	36	11	4	47	17	29	24	35	41					
Sue	Initial sales meetings	12	8	9	4	14	11	15	16	13					
Sue	Proposals (#)	4	2	1	3	4	2	4	5	4					
Sue	Proposals ($)	$300K	$175K	$70K	$275K	$350K	$150K	$370K	$410K	$325K					
Sue	30-day pipeline	$1.5M	$1.15M	$1.05M	$1.10M	$1.25M	$1.15M	$1.05M	$1.10M	$1.25M					
Sue	Contracts (#)	2	2	1	1	2	3	1	3	4					
Sue	Contracts ($)	$150K	$161K	$135K	$75K	$170K	$201K	$41K	$170K	$320K					
Evan	Projects late	1			4	4	4	3	3	4					
Evan	Projects over budget	1							2	2					
Evan	Defects to clients	0		1		1	0	2	1	1					
Evan	Utilization rate	80%		1											
Carol	Cash balance	$75K	$55K	$85K	$70K	$61K	$52K	$91K	$77K	$68K					
Carol	AR > 60 days	< $30K	$42.5	$42.5	$31.0	$26.1	$35.5	$40.5	$34.0	$36.4					
Carol	Billing errors	0	0	1	1	0	0	1	1	0					

ADDITIONAL RESOURCES TO HELP YOU *MEASURE*

- **The Goal**, Eliyahu M. Goldratt
- **Levers**, Amos Schwartzfarb, Trevor Boehm
- **Profit First**, Mike Michalowicz
- **Simple Numbers, Straight Talk, Big Profits!**, Greg Crabtree, Beverly Blair Harzog

FBA CHECKLIST—STEP 3

MANAGE (LMA)	
Who:	Leaders, managers, and supervisors
Facilitated By:	Team Leader, members of Leadership Team
What:	Lead and manage in a way that helps people follow these processes and get better and more consistent results
Summary:	Reinforce behavior change by driving accountability for following the process and getting the desired result
Time:	Ongoing
Result:	LMA (Leadership + Management = Accountability), an EOS Tool
Tools:	The People Analyzer GWC Company Scorecard

STEPS

- Ensure all leaders and managers understand the process and can set clear expectations for compliance, frequency, and outcomes (steps 1 and 2 of the FBA Checklist)
- Monitor Weekly Scorecards, drop off-track numbers to the Issues List
- Hold team members accountable for compliance, frequency, and outcomes on a weekly basis
- Coach and mentor until numbers are being hit consistently
- Ensure you have the right people in the right seats

ADDITIONAL RESOURCES TO HELP YOU *MANAGE (LMA)*

- **How To Be a Great Boss**, Gino Wickman, René Boer
- **Traction**, Gino Wickman
- **The One-Minute Manager Meets the Monkey**, Kenneth Blanchard, William Oncken Jr., Hal Burrows
- **The Five Dysfunctions of a Team**, Patrick Lencioni
- **Radical Candor**, Kim Scott

FBA CHECKLIST—STEP 4

UPDATE	
Who:	Owner of each core process
Facilitated By:	Team Leader or Process Champion
What:	Review and update processes at least annually
Summary:	Review process annually (or more frequently if necessary). Look for ways to streamline, automate, adjust to, and anticipate a changing industry, market, and world
Time:	Ongoing
Result:	Reviewed and/or updated core processes
Tools:	The 3-Step Process Documenter

STEPS

- Schedule a recurring appointment to review each core process (e.g., quarterly or annually)
- When prompted, set an individual Rock to complete this project
- Take note of changes in the world, your industry, and the market into which you sell
- Take note of any technological advancements that have occurred since the prior update. Does new equipment or better software exist that would allow you to streamline or automate the process?
- With those observations made, follow step 2 of the 3-Step Process Documenter
  - Observe
  - Evaluate
  - Document and Simplify
  - Get Leadership Team approval for the updated process
  - Restart the FBA Checklist

ADDITIONAL RESOURCES TO HELP YOU UPDATE

- **Who Moved My Cheese?**, Spencer Johnson, MD
- **The Four Lenses of Innovation**, Rowan Gibson
- **Switch, How to Change Things When Change Is Hard**, Chip Heath, Dan Heath
- **The Innovator's Dilemma**, Clayton M. Christensen

PULLING IT ALL TOGETHER

THE STRONG *PROCESS!* CHECKLIST

When you can check each box below, your organization is at least 80% strong in the Process Component:

1. We are all fully **committed** to keeping our Process Component strong. ☐

2. We have **identified** our handful of core processes. ☐

3. We have **documented and simplified** each of them by ☐
   - observing how we do things now
   - evaluating what we observe and looking for ways to improve
   - simplifying the process
   - documenting the major steps in the process

4. Our leadership team has **reviewed and approved** each core process. ☐

5. We **package** our core processes so that each of them is easy to find and use. ☐

6. We **train** everyone who touches even one step in each core process. ☐

7. We **measure** compliance, frequency, or outcomes when and where it makes sense. ☐

8. We **manage** people well, to drive accountability for following each core process. ☐

9. We **update** each process at least annually and then restart the FBA Checklist. ☐

10. We are consistently getting the **results** we want. ☐

CONCLUSION

Magic?

Perhaps not. Strengthening your Process Component may be simple, but it requires commitment, learning, and plenty of hard work. Nearly all of the leaders with whom we've worked—thousands of gifted, hard-working people—struggled at some point in the journey to strengthen their organization's Process Component. Every single one of them would tell you, however, that the journey was worth it. If you're not getting everything you want from your business, we're confident you will feel the same way.

Consider the remodeling contractor who rose from the ashes to rebuild his business and live his ideal life. Learn from the owner of the home services business who reignited growth, increased profit, and built a facility and culture he and his family can be proud of. Think of the founders who sold at high multiples to very experienced buyers and were told, "This is the best-run business we've ever seen." Be inspired by the Visionary owner whose passion for early childhood education done the right way has turned into an amazing business that's expanding regionally.

These leaders are very much like you. They are visionaries, builders, disruptors, and freedom seekers who started a business with passion, drive, and a desire to make a difference in the world. They thrive on creativity, adaptability, and speed. And yet, every one of these leaders built their businesses, and their lives, on a firm foundation of process. They did the work described in this book, and you can too.

So please, get started right away. Though it may seem paradoxical, process *will* set you and your business free. If this book helps you do just that and begins reigniting the passion leaders around the world have for their businesses, that's magic enough for us.

ACKNOWLEDGMENTS

This book would not have been possible without the influence, guidance, and help of so many people, including those we have listed below. We will never be able to thank you enough for your impact on our lives, our work, and this book.

OUR EOS COMMUNITY AND
OTHER KEY CONTRIBUTORS

Gino Wickman, your passion for helping entrepreneurs live their ideal lives has inspired us to do the same. Thanks for creating an amazing set of simple and practical tools and deciding to share them with the world. We've been the happy beneficiaries of that decision, as have the hundreds of EOS Implementers, and the thousands of entrepreneurs around the world that work with these tools every day. Finally, thanks for helping us make this book simple, clear, and useful, and for making the two of us better facilitators, teachers, and coaches.

Don Tinney, thank you for building the EOS Implementer Community into something we both love being a part of every day.

You've taught us to see each client and colleague as a masterpiece, and to teach with grace, patience, and a genuine desire to help.

Matthew Carnicelli, Jennifer DeBrow, Drew Robinson, John Paine, Glenn Yeffeth, and the exceptional team at BenBella Books, we're eternally grateful for your help bringing this book to life, making the journey enjoyable, and pushing it over the finish line.

Thank you, especially, to the worldwide EOS Implementer Community. It's an honor to call you all friends and colleagues. We're grateful to have so many talented, abundance-minded people with us on this lifelong journey to mastery. We wrote this book to help you teach these principles consistently and with confidence, and to help your clients benefit more profoundly from the work you do together.

A special thank you to those implementers who offered inspiration, suggestions, test-reader feedback, client introductions, and other valuable material for this book: Mike Abercrombie, Eric Albertson, Matt Beecher, Ken Bogard, Hugo Boutet, Walt Brown, Christian Bruns, Jim Bygland, Victoria Cabot, Lorie Clements, Jim Coyle, Will Crist, CJ Dubé, Ben Goetz, John Gross, Matt Hahne, Michael Halperin, Sue Hawkes, Andrea Jones, Sonya Jury, Angela Kalemis, Mike Kotsis, Cyrus Lemon, Jeremy Macliver, Aaron Marcum, Gabby Matzdorf, Dennis McCluskey, Randy McDougal, Sandi Mitchell, Hank O'Donnell, Mark O'Donnell, Scott Patchin, Joe Paulsen, Shea Peffly, Erik Perkins, Jaime Robertson-Lavalle, Laurel Romanella, Dean Russell, Don Sasse, Ann Sheu, Pinches Shmaya, Bill Stratton, Jeanet Wade, Jeff Whittle, Mike Wolfgang, Nate Wolfson, Shelly Woodson, and Jill Young.

Finally, thank you to the business owners and leaders whose generosity, honesty, and vulnerability has made *Process!* exponentially better: Bret Abbot, Jackie Chodl, and Kate Silbernick; Julie

Allinson; Bell Alic and Chris Ronzio; Robert Artigues; Jerry Baak and Mary Jayne Crocker; Richard Bahr; Peter Bonfe; Mike Campbell; Chris Carlson; Dodd Clasen; Patrick Condon, Matt Hennebry, Jenny Gonzales, Kellie Herring, and Mike Miller; Brian Strandes; Ryan Diekow and Nicole Hovorson; Andrew Duneman and Ryan Batcheller; Andre Durand; Alister Esam; Jeff Fritz; Shea Hickman; Peter Holtgreive; Julia Lindley; Jon LoDuca; Matt Meents; Kory MacGregor and Alice Gascho; Ali Nasser and Melissa Bushman; Erik Piasio; David Reiling, Hannah Heinze, and Mike Porcello; David Reuter; Garry Ridge; Jere Simpson; Jason Smylie; Natalie Standridge; Eric Unger; and Gary Vanbutsele.

PATON'S FAMILY AND FRIENDS

Dearest Kate, your presence in my life is a gift I'll treasure forever. You make me a better person, our family safe and well-loved, and our home the sanctuary we imagined it could be—all with a great sense of humor and amazing grace. My true and perfect partner.

Jon, thanks for loving your old man despite all of his obvious flaws. You've become a wonderful man and an exceptional entrepreneur—I couldn't be more proud of you. Henry, you are the most courageous person I know. My hope for you is that you learn to be as confident in yourself and your future as Kate and I are. We see who you really are and what you're capable of. And Charlie, where do I even begin? Your smile lights up a room. Your love of learning and story-telling has inspired me. And you're so kind you even (occasionally) laugh at my jokes. Michael and Jack, thank you for welcoming me into your family, and for reminding me how to live life to the fullest and overcome adversity. Your futures are bright, and I look forward to enjoying them with you.

Mom, Pop, Hester, Ozzie, and Lisa—thanks for creating a sense of family, safety, and belonging when it wasn't easy. Thank you for instilling in me a love for learning and a passion for helping and teaching others.

To that end, a hearty thank you to my teachers and friends over the years: Steve and Mark Hatch, Laura Casale, Kay Shutler, Dave Radanovich, Jack Thomas, Chip Letzgus, David Anderson, Phil Martin, George Thompson, Lisa Phillips, Martha Ford, Amy Eddings, David Gibbs, Carl Phillips, Barbara Rigney, Tom Green, Betsy Lloyd, Kyle Smith, Pam Archer, Vince Simonetti, Tom Thon, John Cocumelli, Rick Simonton, Brett and Katie Kauffman, Dodd and Sharon Clasen, Billie and Sue McCarthy, and Susan Broadwell. My heart is full because of the impact you (and countless others whose names escape me at this moment) have had on my life.

To all my EOS Clients and talk sponsors—thank you for your trust and confidence. I genuinely love the work I do, the people with and for whom I do it, and the life I'm able to live. None of that would be possible without you.

To April Sonksen, Kristen McLinden, and Kristen Pryzbilla—thank you for being great people and working together to make us a great team. I'm blessed to have you in my life.

LISA'S FAMILY AND FRIENDS

From weekly family meetings to charts and games, thank you to my family for playing along. Paddy, being on our personal and professional journey together has been life's greatest blessing. Thank you for inviting me into your life, your business, and for supporting my growth. I am thrilled that EOS has given you the freedom to pursue your passion for helping entrepreneurs Build Joy!

Donny, you bring excellence to everything you do. As you head to college, enjoy it all! Thank you for being such an amazing role model and leader. Alex, thank you for your honesty, curiosity, and humor. I am so proud of the intentional life that you live. Skybear, thank you for being the missing puzzle piece in our lives and for bringing such joy, compassion, and fun to everything that you do. God's got this!

My parents and siblings, Annie, Al, and Marco, thank you for showing me the power of perseverance and opportunity. Our life experiences have given me the compassion and focus to help entrepreneurs everywhere reach their goals.

Tracy Sieve and Farida Djaelani, thank you for keeping the plates spinning and for supporting me and our clients each day.

Finally, to my fabulous clients, you inspire me daily with your commitment to doing the work. The impact you make on your employees' lives goes beyond your business. I am honored to be in the room with you. You are the reason I do this work.

ABOUT THE AUTHORS

Mike Paton has spent every working day of the last fifteen years helping thousands of leaders around the globe run better businesses and live better lives. An EOS Implementer and sought-after speaker, Paton co-authored *Get A Grip* with Gino Wickman, spent five years as the Visionary for EOS Worldwide, and is the host of the top-rated podcast *The EOS Leader*. He now spends all his time giving back by helping others master the timeless disciplines and practical tools you'll read about in *Process!* and the other books in the Traction Library.

Lisa González has dedicated her career to helping businesses achieve their goals. After testing different business principles in an entrepreneurial company, she read *Traction* and implemented its practical tools. EOS made such a profound impact in *every* aspect of the business that Lisa committed to sharing it with other growth-minded companies. Today, as an EOS Implementer, she is thrilled to help other entrepreneurs get what they want from their businesses and lives. Lisa graduated from UCLA and The University of Texas School of Law. She is a past member of Vistage, EO, and a past board member of YPO.

GET A GRIP

An Entrepreneurial Fable: Your Journey to Get Real, Get Simple, and Get Results

by Gino Wickman and Mike Paton

Learn more at